Nonprofit Management Simplified

Board and Volunteer Development

Marilyn L. Donnellan, MS

Nonprofit Management Simplified: Board and Volunteer Development

One of the **Nonprofit Management Simplified**™ series

Published by
CharityChannel Press, an imprint of CharityChannel LLC
424 Church Street, Suite 2000
Nashville, TN 37219 USA

CharityChannel.com

ISBN Print Book: 978-1-938077-82-1

Library of Congress Control Number: 2016943356

13 12 11 10 9 8 7 6 5 4 3 2 1

Printed in the United States of America

This and most CharityChannel Press books are available at special quantity discounts for bulk purchases for sales promotions, premiums, fundraising, or educational use. For information, contact CharityChannel Press, 424 Church Street, Suite 2000, Nashville, TN 37219 USA. +1 949-589-5938.

Publisher's Acknowledgments

This book was produced by a team dedicated to excellence; please send your feedback to Editors@CharityChannel.com.

We first wish to acknowledge the tens of thousands of peers who call *charitychannel.com* their online professional home. Your enthusiastic support for the **Nonprofit Management Simplified** series is the wind in our sails.

Members of the team who produced this book include:

Editors

Acquisitions: Linda Lysakowski

Comprehensive Editing: Linda Lysakowski

Copy Editing: Joy Metcalf

Production

Layout: Joy Metcalf

Illustrations: Kim O'Reilly

Design: Stephen Nill

Administrative

CharityChannel LLC: Stephen Nill, CEO

Marketing and Public Relations: John Millen

About the Author

Marilyn L. Donnellan, MS, fortuitously fell into nonprofit management when the editor of the newspaper where she was working as a reporter suggested she apply for the executive director position of a small nonprofit. Over the next twenty-plus years, she enthusiastically served in five nonprofits, ranging in size from that single staff organization with a $150,000 budget to one with three hundred staff and a $6 million budget. She figured it out along the way, collecting tons of resources to help her with the myriad responsibilities and challenges.

When her stack of resources got too large to fit in a filing cabinet, Donnellan decided to open a consulting firm to share what she had learned with other nonprofit staff. She has been a consultant for more than ten years, helping hundreds of nonprofits build their capacity; although her filing cabinet is still bursting at the seams.

Donnellan is the author of three books on nonprofit management: *Core Elements of a Successful Nonprofit, The Hour Series of Guides for Nonprofit Management,* and *The Complete Guide to Church Management.* She has authored articles in *The Nonprofit Times* and *The Nonprofit Digest.* Her award-winning helps for nonprofits are in use around the world. Her latest book, *Two Faces of Me,* is an autobiographical account of her experiences with Sophie Longhoofer, a bag-lady character she often personifies in her public speaking.

Dedication

To Steve, the love of my life, who believes I can do anything and is always there for support, even if it means him sacrificing a round of golf.

Author's Acknowledgments

I could never in a million years have imagined that this farm girl from Oregon would one day be a published author. Special thanks go to the board members, staff, and volunteers at all those nonprofits where I served, who patiently taught me so much about what it means to be an excellent manager and how to balance passion with expertise.

Thank you fellow consultants and clients who encouraged me to keep on writing and who shared so much of your own experiences so I could do my job better.

Thank you, Scott Bechtler-Levin, formerly of Ideaencore/4Good. You encouraged me to try new methods of marketing. The dozens of consultants and executive directors who reviewed the manuscripts, in spite of their busy schedules, deserve special thanks and kudos. And deep appreciation to everyone at CharityChannel, led by the able Stephen Nill, who enthusiastically encouraged my creativity.

Contents

Summary of Chapters

Board Development. Training board members on their roles, responsibilities, and lines of authority in their relationships with staff is a critical strategy for effective nonprofit management. Organizational, governance, and committee structures are overviewed. The rationale for board training and effective strategies for the recruitment, orientation, recognition, and dismissal of board members are also included.

Simplified Strategic Planning. "We do not have time to plan" can no longer be an excuse for lack of strategic planning. This award-winning, simplified strategy for strategic planning is ideal for board members and executive directors who are new to strategic planning. The process includes strategies for adapting to unexpected changes in the nonprofit's environment in between annual planning sessions.

Effective Meetings. Boring, long meetings are often the norm in nonprofits. This chapter overviews the strategies related to facilitating a meeting, the agenda, minutes, and how their effective use can reduce the length and boredom of all types of meetings.

Executive Director Performance Reviews. The hiring, supervision, and dismissal of the Executive Director (ED) are board responsibilities. An effective ED performance review, conducted by the board chair or a designated task force, removes the subjectivity and focuses on board-approved core competencies on which the ED job description and performance review are based.

The Executive Director Report to the Board. Regular reports by the ED to the board are critical, not only for keeping the board informed, but also to help the ED better manage time and priorities. A daily system of recordkeeping can simplify and improve the ED's reports.

Volunteer Development. Strategies and policies for the recruitment, orientation, recognition, and dismissal for all three types of volunteers (board, committee, and program) are overviewed, along with sample policies and templates that are easily adaptable to any nonprofit.

Foreword

Perhaps no nonprofit relationship holds as much potential promise (or peril) as that between a nonprofit executive director (ED) and the board in general and the board chair specifically. This is especially so when the ED or the board chair is new to the role in that particular organization. And yet, far too often, that relationship evolves in a manner that leaves maximum impact unrealized or—worse yet—needless and distracting issues arise that create dysfunction.

Now comes Marilyn Donnellan with a thoughtful and practical guide to bringing your board/ED relationship to a much better place. *Nonprofit Management Simplified: Board and Volunteer Development* lays out a comprehensive approach that can greatly assist you in learning and profiting from the experiences—good and bad—of those who have preceded you in the sector.

As is the case with her other volumes in the *Nonprofit Management Simplified* series, *Board and Volunteer Development* is grounded in everyday reality while simultaneously tying those daily realities to their strategic implications. Her advice is practical, the tools she provides useful, and her voice of experience essential. She's an experienced practitioner on many nonprofit fronts—ED, board member, and consulting "guru"—from small startup to multimillion nonprofit organizations. She'll have you seeing around corners so as to avoid the avoidable and be well prepared to address the unexpected.

Board and Volunteer Development deserves to be a go-to resource whether you are new to the nonprofit sector or an experienced veteran mentoring up-and-coming staff or a new board member. Read it cover to cover; revisit it often.

Time is the one resource that most of us never seem to have enough of. The time you'll save by putting its principles into practice can then be better spent on performing those mission-driven actions that you (and, in some cases, only you) can do best to improve your organization's impact. Marilyn has laid out a strategically significant roadmap. It is up to you to actually put it into play.

The nonprofit sector does not lack vision. The trick is how best to translate that vision into appropriate actions that result in real impact. A Japanese proverb says it best: "Vision without action is a daydream. Action without vision is a nightmare."

Board and Volunteer Development can be an exceptionally useful vehicle in helping to bring your nonprofit's impact "dream" to fruition. I also strongly encourage you to take advantage of the insights and practical tools Marilyn offers in all the volumes of her *Nonprofit Management Simplified* series.

Jack Flanagan,
Founder, Center for Effective Nonprofit Governance and Management

Introduction

I am convinced that the executive director (ED) who starts a career as the only staff person in a very small nonprofit has a distinct advantage over the EDs of large organizations.

Why? Because when you are the only staff person you are forced to learn everything there is to know about everything. When I finally had staff to help with the myriad responsibilities, my experiences at the small nonprofit greatly enhanced my staff management capabilities: I knew exactly what these jobs entailed; I had done them myself.

I remember early in my nonprofit career thinking that maybe I should take a class on marketing. But the reality was I did not have any spare hours to take the class. So, I burned the midnight oil reading, attended a periodic workshop, and then just figured it out on my own, striving to break down all of the management responsibilities into their simplest and most workable strategies.

I know you do not have the time or the energy to spend weeks or months learning an accounting system or putting together a sophisticated fundraising or marketing plan. Every day you are must balance and prioritize all the core elements that make for a successful nonprofit.

The three handbooks in this series do not examine the philosophical or theoretical issues of nonprofit management. Instead, the information simplifies nonprofit management by breaking it down into the core elements, providing proven and workable strategies. Field-tested policies, templates, checklists, and procedures are included for every topic.

Nonprofit Management Simplified: Internal Operations focuses on all things administrative: finances, personnel management, risk management, starting a nonprofit, assessments, and plain, old-fashioned time management.

Nonprofit Management Simplified: Board and Volunteer Development includes everything you need to know about board governance, strategic planning, ED performance reviews, and the recruitment, training, recognition, and dismissal of all three types of volunteers: board, committee, and program.

Nonprofit Management Simplified: Programs and Fundraising outlines tools and strategies for developing and assessing the programs from an outcomes measurements approach. Community involvement, marketing, and all types of resource development strategies are examined, with assessment strategies for each element included.

Chapter One

Board Development

IN THIS CHAPTER

···→ Rationale for board development

···→ The roles and responsibilities of board and staff

···→ Governance, organizational structures, and committees for boards

···→ Recruitment and training, recognition, and dismissal strategies

When I first started in nonprofit management, I saw board members as roadblocks to my efforts. "I could get so much more done if it weren't for my board members," a colleague complained to me.

"I know what you mean," I replied. "The board members just get in my way." I have to admit—it took me a few years before I got it through my thick skull that board members can be one of the most valuable assets I have as the executive director.

So how can you move away from viewing the board as meddling to one of your best assets to support your efforts?

Building an effective board is critical to your ability to do your job as the executive director (ED), not only because a governing board is mandated by legal authorities but because their enthusiasm and passion can have a profound impact on achievement of the nonprofit's mission. But if you are like most nonprofit EDs, you have had little training on how to work effectively with a board.

Conflicts between board members and staff are not unusual. But if you, your staff, and your board members have been trained in the various hats or roles of board members, there will be less conflict and more goal achievement. And board members are less apt to overstep their legal roles and move into meddling with your responsibilities.

An enthusiastic, talented, and experienced staff person was assigned the task of developing and running a nonprofit's first golf tournament fundraiser. One of the board members volunteered to be the honorary chairperson of the tournament.

After the successful tournament, the staff person was fired. When the bewildered staff person asked the ED why she was being fired, she replied, "Because the board member told me you did not follow her directions."

This is a perfect example of what can happen when neither the board member nor the ED understand the proper roles, responsibilities, and lines of authority for board and staff.

 stories from the real world

Board Development Philosophies

I frequently hear nonprofit professionals refer to their work with the board of directors as "board management." But consider the differences in perception between the terms "board management" and "board development."

"Management" can carry a connotation of manipulation, while "development" is a more strengthening concept. If you rethink your critical work with the board of directors as a strategy to strengthen your efforts, as well as to improve the organization, the approach will enhance your own efficiency and effectiveness.

There are three distinct philosophies or attitudes which illustrate the strategies most often used when working with nonprofit boards.

Controlling

The controlling philosophy is particularly common among nonprofit professionals who come from a government or military background and who lack nonprofit board development training. Since they are not quite sure what to do with the board, controlling executives implement strategies to manipulate or control the board so the things to be accomplished can be done without board meddling—in other words, assigning busy work to the board and asking the board to simply rubber stamp all the executive's recommendations.

Coasting

The most common philosophy of board management is "coasting." This philosophy is based on the reality that neither executive nor board members understand their roles, so they coast along as best they can, often being swayed by the strongest voice or by a staff or board member, whether right or wrong. Neither board members nor the executive are willing to admit they do not know their roles, resulting in frequent frustration and power struggles.

Courageous

Good board development fits into the courageous philosophy because it takes courage on your part to let the board lead the nonprofit in governance, strategic planning, and policy setting. It takes courage for you, your staff, and board members to take the time to understand clearly what the roles and lines of authority are and then to work together to fulfill the mission of the nonprofit. It also takes courage and trust for board members to let go of the details and let you do what you were hired to do.

Volunteer Roles in a Nonprofit

There are basically three roles for volunteers in any nonprofit: serving on the board, serving on a committee, or serving as a program volunteer.

Board of Directors

Members of the board are usually recruited for their passion or commitment to the mission of the nonprofit because they represent a specific stakeholder or because their community leadership or

After decades of exemplary work with a national association, the chief executive officer (CEO) was indicted on dozens of felony charges. Members of the association were appalled at what the indictment said about his behavior with staff and his illegal use of association funds.

At an informal meeting of the association members after the indictment, one of the disgraced CEO's administrative staff told the group the CEO was extremely manipulative of the board.

"If there was a controversial issue that was going to be brought before the board at the next meeting," the staffer said, "the CEO would call each of the board members to get their opinions on the issue. He would also ask them what dates would work for them for the next board meeting. Once he knew which board members disagreed with his view on the issue, the CEO would purposely schedule the meeting for when those disagreeing board members were not going to be able to attend."

That's what I call a controlling executive!

 stories from the real world

financial contribution can be a source of help to the nonprofit.

The primary roles of a board member are to legally govern the nonprofit through thoughtful and workable policy setting, monitoring policy and program implementation, strategic planning, executive director oversight, financial oversight, public relations, and fundraising.

Committee Volunteers

Volunteers who act in an advisory role to board-level standing committees or task forces bring a high degree of expertise in a specific area. A marketing committee, for example, could be composed of volunteers with marketing and/or media background and experience. While their recommendations may eventually trigger a board policy, the committee volunteer's primary role is to advise the staff. And the staff's role is to advise members of the committee. Advisory boards are in the same category as committee volunteers.

Program Volunteers

Many volunteers perform duties which might ordinarily be done by staff. The multitude of program volunteers in the nonprofit community serve food at soup kitchens, babysit for young mothers who need some time off, develop and run fundraising events, or any of myriad other activities on which the nonprofit depends. The primary role of a program volunteer is to support the programs of the organization.

How Do These Different Roles Function Within a Nonprofit?

Confusion often arises when a board member is serving in all three capacities or roles. The development of board-approved policies related to the recruitment, training, dismissal, and recognition of all volunteers, including board members, is essential to reducing confusion and increasing effectiveness of everyone involved with the nonprofit.

Although this chapter focuses on board development, many of the examples, templates, and suggestions can be adapted to any type of volunteer. **Chapter Six** includes templates and suggestions for volunteer development policies and procedures specifically related to recruitment, training, dismissal, and recognition of non-board members.

Types of Boards

There are generally five types of boards operating within the nonprofit sector and defined by their function: governing, advisory, administrative, transitional, and institutional. As shown in the Board Functions table later in the chapter, the type of board and style of governance chosen depends not only on the size of the nonprofit but also on where it is in the stages of organizational development. The number and types of committees will also depend on these factors.

Unfortunately, it is the rare nonprofit that carefully and regularly evaluates what type of board they are, their governance structure, and the committees they really should have. These important issues are seemingly answered by osmosis, with neither board members nor staff knowing enough to make conscious decisions.

Governing Board

Generally, the governing board is the entity defined by the government as legally responsible for setting and monitoring policy for private nonprofits. Laws related to their functions may be different in countries outside the United States, so check with the proper governmental authorities before developing your board training strategies.

A governing board in the United States makes policy decisions regarding purposes (mission), functions (programs), and goals (planning). Such a board also hires and evaluates the ED, who is responsible to the board. Having a governing board is a requirement by the Internal Revenue Service (IRS) for any 501(c)(3) nonprofit.

The various types of governance structures will be discussed later in the chapter.

Advisory Boards

Advisory boards are found in both private nonprofits and governments. The advisory board primarily gives advice and makes recommendations to the governing board and staff but have no legal authority. The ED is not appointed by the advisory board or responsible to it and does not have to follow their advice.

Larger or international nonprofits might develop advisory boards to serve various geographical areas. Advisory boards should more properly be called advisory committees or advisory task forces since they have no governing authority.

Unfortunately, since advisory board members are not often trained to know that their sole function is advice, not governance, members will sometimes inappropriately dabble in governance issues. This action can create some real but unnecessary headaches for everyone involved.

Administrative

Nonprofit start-up boards are often administrative boards, meaning they are a group of volunteers who have joined together to establish programs to address a particular need. They usually act as unpaid staff (but can receive a temporary salary as long as they avoid conflicts of interest) and do everything from running programs to doing the bookkeeping until the first staff is hired.

Administrative board members carry out their own policies through administrative activities. Such a board makes decisions regarding both programs and policies and is also regarded by the IRS as the governing board.

Transitional Boards

Keep in mind, however, that many times a nonprofit will, out of necessity, change or add to the board's responsibilities. For example, the governing board of a small nonprofit whose ED has resigned could temporarily move back into an administrative role. These types of boards could also be called transitional boards since they adapt to changes in the nonprofit by revising their roles to fit the nonprofit's needs.

Problems often arise with administrative boards of start-up nonprofits when they hire their first paid staff. Used to doing everything from administration duties to legal governance, board members can have a difficult time focusing only on governance when the staff is hired. Sometimes the only effective way to deal with this transition problem is to replace the original board members with individuals who are trained solely in governance.

Institutional Boards

Large hospitals, universities, and foundations will often have institutional boards. These boards do very little governing or administrative work and are sometimes, although rarely, paid for their work on the board.

Sample job descriptions for the three primary types of nonprofit boards (administrative, governing, and advisory) are included as **Appendix A**.

Not only are governing boards a requirement in the United States for any 501(c)(3) nonprofit, but well-trained boards can have a profound, positive impact on your nonprofit. IRS guidelines state that nonprofits exist solely for the purpose of public benefit versus private, individual gain. Board members, in essence, own the nonprofit.

John Carver, author of *Boards That Make a Difference*, says: "Governing boards. . . do not exist to help staff but to own the business." He also says the most important function of a governing board is setting policy.

> I was consulting with an ED who had founded a nonprofit. As I questioned him about where the organization was in their stage of development, I asked a couple of questions:
>
> ◆ Do board members have term limits?
>
> ◆ Is the ED a voting member of the board?
>
> The answers to the questions told me a lot about what governance stage they were in. He replied that no, there were no term limits, and yes, the ED was a voting member.
>
> His answers indicated to me that the organization was still in the start-up governance phase. The founder and ED was afraid to let go of governance control so board members were primarily family members with no term limits and he still had a vote.
>
> Until he was willing to relinquish control, the nonprofit could get stuck in the start-up governance phase.
>
> **Example**

Types of Governance Structures and Board-Level Committees

In the same way that there are different types of boards (start-up, administrative, governing, institutional, advisory), there are different models or types of governance structures. Depending on where the nonprofit is in its development stage will usually determine which governance structure will work best. Unfortunately, boards can get stuck in one type of governance structure, not knowing they need to move to a different one.

Professionals in the nonprofit sector have wide ranging opinions on the number and types of governance structures, but until a nonprofit identifies which one they are in, it will be difficult to establish a good board-level committee structure or move to the next phase of organizational development. Examples of governance structures include the following:

Start-up or Advisor Governance Structure

In this type of governance, the founder is usually a voting member of the board and eventually becomes the paid ED. Board members primarily serve as advisors to the ED and are recruited primarily because the ED trusts them. Often the board members are also family members, and there are no term limits.

This type of governance structure might work well for a short period of time, but if it continues too long, it could expose the organization to significant legal risk. This is because board members usually do not know about or understand their legal governance responsibilities, leaving everything up to the founder/ED.

Donor-based Governance Structure

Primarily composed of high-end donors to the organization, this type of structure is based on the recruitment of board members totally based on how much they donate. There is often little or no governance role, creating even greater legal liability than in the start-up type of structure. Often the ED tightly controls who comes on the board and when they leave the board.

Board Functions Chart

Budget Size of Nonprofit	Number of Paid Staff	Type of Board	Governance Strategy	Committees
Up to $150,000	0–1	Administrative	Start-up or advisor	Most of the procedural work is done at the board level, with task forces as needed, with a finance committee meeting monthly. These are often start-up nonprofits.
$150,000 to $1 million	2–5	Administrative or governance	Cooperative, administrative, team, or committee	Because there are few staff, the board often relies on a complicated committee process to develop policies and procedures.
$1 million to $3 million	5–12	Governance or translational	Cooperative, team, or committee	Although there is more staff, it is sometimes difficult for these boards to move away from a complicated committee process and dealing with administrative issues.
$3 million to $6 million	12–30	Governance or translational	Team or committee	More apt to deal primarily with governance issues, there will still be some reliance on up to six board-level committees.
$6 million and up	30 and up	Governance or institutional	Donor, advisor, legal, or policy	Simply because of the size of the nonprofit, and depending on the strength of the CEO, the board will focus on legal governance and policy issues or retreat to primarily donor-driven or advisor roles. Committees are rare since staff do everything.

Cooperative or Administrative Governance Structure

Governed without paid staff, this type of structure is often found in start-up organizations but will only last if there are enough qualified volunteers to do everything needed. This structure depends heavily on board-level committees who handle virtually every administrative task, reporting to the board on what they have done.

This can work well initially but can quickly create burnout in the volunteers and move the board away from legal governance to what I call "counting paper clips" or the minutiae of management.

Team or Committee Governance Structure

These types of boards are often ideal for small to mid-sized nonprofits with small staff. The board's committee structure mirrors the functions of the organization (fundraising, marketing, finances, etc.).

The board's primary duties are legal governance, but they regularly review reports from the board-level committees, where policies are developed and brought to the board for approval.

Term limits are usually present, and the ED generally does not have a vote at board meetings. Unless the board chair is properly trained in meeting facilitation, it is easy for the board meetings to become primarily committee reports.

Legal or Policy Governance Structure

Generally found in large nonprofits, these boards are the most sophisticated in their governance, focusing primarily on their legal governance responsibilities.

Unfortunately, too often in this type of structure, a strong ED (usually called a CEO at this level) can exert too much control on board members. If board members are not properly trained in their legal governance responsibilities, they can become lax in their attention to their duties.

No matter where your nonprofit is in their organizational development, it is a good idea to periodically establish a governance committee or task force to carefully review which governance structure the nonprofit is currently using and if there is a need to change to a different structure. Regardless of the structure the organization is using, there is often confusion on not only how many committees a board should have but also how they operate. The details of conducting effective board and committee meetings are included in **Chapter Three**. Organizational and committee structure will be dealt with later in this chapter.

Everything the board does must revolve around policy clarification as the central feature of board leadership. Policy setting then becomes the parameter within which any strategic plan, any staff work, and any board meeting must operate.

It will help you greatly if you view board development as one of the most critical responsibilities you have as an ED. A well-trained board can be a tremendous asset to you, not only because they "own" the nonprofit but also because they can be a repository of a wealth of information, expertise, and experience, especially if you are an executive new to the community.

Board Members' Roles and Responsibilities

There are five critical governance responsibilities of nonprofit boards in the United States:

- ◆ legal compliance
- ◆ policy setting
- ◆ financial oversight
- ◆ ED oversight
- ◆ strategic planning

You may need to change this list of board responsibilities to correspond to your country's legal requirements.

There are three additional board member responsibilities which are supportive of the organization:

- ◆ public relations
- ◆ fundraising
- ◆ self-assessment

Legal Compliance

The legal responsibilities for board members are based on two specific legal statements and four duties:

◆ the reasonably prudent person

◆ the principle of good faith

◆ duty of obedience

◆ duty of care

◆ duty of loyalty

◆ duty of transparency

Board members can be held legally liable if they fail to adhere to these legal principles. Whenever legal issues arise related to nonprofits, the legal process used by the courts includes a review of how the board members acted in relationship to these two statements as well as every board member's level of fulfillment of the four duties.

Legal Responsibilities

The reasonably prudent person avoids:	The principle of good faith says board members shall:
Mismanagement: doing things the wrong way	Attend all meetings
Nonmanagement: not doing required things	Know about the nonprofit and what will be discussed
Self-dealing: decisions based on personal gain	Ensure the nonprofit meets all legal and technical requirements
	Record "no" votes at board and committee meetings to prevent personal liability
	Avoid undermining the mission of the nonprofit and avoid self-dealing
Principles of Duty	**Definition**
Duty of obedience	Obedience to the central purposes which guide decisions and that the organization functions within the law, governments, and its own bylaws and policies
Duty of care	Oversight of financial matters, reading of minutes, attention to issues and raising questions whenever something is unclear or questionable
Duty of loyalty	Avoid conflicts of interest or appearance of conflicts of interest, including conflicts with other organizations with which a board member is involved
Duty of transparency	Transparency in operations; for example, filing of IRS Form 990 and other appropriate information and tax returns required to be made public and always being open with all stakeholders and the public on finances, overhead costs, fundraising costs, senior staff salaries, etc.

Your board members have a legal responsibility to make sure the nonprofit is always in full compliance with all local, state, and federal requirements and that required reports to governmental agencies are filed in a timely manner. At new board member orientations and at least annually, board members need to be reminded of their legal responsibilities and the principles of obedience, care, duty, and transparency.

Policy Setting

Although policy development is the primary responsibility of a board of directors, few board members clearly understand what policy is. If you educate your board on the specifics of policy development, they will be less apt to make you the target when there are problems. Policy, in its simplest terms, is a specific principle which becomes the framework for action for staff procedures. Board manuals are a great tool for board members to use when making policy decisions.

Good policies delegate authority and become a way to develop plans. Policies are always written down and are never final. Policies can change as the needs of the organization change.

Policies answer the question, "why?" For example, a board might develop two policies related to development of the nonprofit's budget:

◆ "Expenses will not exceed revenue."

◆ "The ED has the authority to negotiate and sign contracts under $5,000, but the board will be notified within thirty days of any contract signed."

If the board is doing their job of governing by policy, you and your staff will clearly understand the framework within which they can or cannot work in any given situation.

Good policies govern *why* programs are implemented. Policy does not establish *what* programs are implemented but guides the overarching governing strategies on how they are implemented: the big picture, not the details.

Strategic Planning

Board members are responsible for making sure the nonprofit is doing regular planning. More information on this issue is contained in **Chapter Two**.

Financial Oversight

Your board members have a responsibility to make sure the nonprofit is adhering to all of the necessary financial management policies and procedures. The US standards of accounting (*fasb.org*) include benchmarks board members can use to make sure the nonprofit is fiscally sound. There are also international accounting standards. Chapter three

---

Board manuals or board reference books can be used for orientation of new board members (either online or printed versions). A frequently updated manual can also be a handy tool during board meetings when questions are raised about issues like mission, strategic plan, programs, bylaws, etc. Additionally, to reduce legal risks, all board members should know about or have the following in their board manuals:

◆ list of current board members and their committee assignments

◆ list of current staff and copies of their job descriptions

◆ copy of organizational articles of incorporation or charter, and bylaws

◆ copy of most recent financial reports, policies, accounting procedures, and audits

◆ copy of recent reports to funding sources and a list of all funding sources

◆ minutes of recent board meetings

◆ copy of staff personnel policies and any other board-approved policies

◆ copies of any special reports or analyses done on the nonprofit, such as the strategic plan

◆ updates on current programs and projects

◆ organizational chart

Example

of *Nonprofit Management Simplified: Internal Operations* includes examples and templates for all of the internal controls and policies mentioned in this chapter.

While it is your responsibility as the ED to monitor and execute financial strategies and policies, board members must understand they have a legal and ethical responsibility to periodically review the financial management policies and the accounting system. It is unusual for lawsuits against nonprofits and their boards to be successful if board members have periodically assured themselves all financial aspects of the organization are in order.

Board members can get a report on the internal financial processes by having the volunteer treasurer, or other board officer, to at least annually do an internal audit. A finance committee, or a subcommittee of the administration committee, can play a key role in holding staff accountable for the financial controls.

By also using a financial checklist, the committee or individual board members can assure themselves the proper policies are in place and being followed by designated staff. Mini-orientations for board members could include an overview of financial processes and policies as well as training on how to understand financial reports and audits.

The board is responsible for hiring an independent auditor. It is your responsibility as the ED to compile and provide the board with a list of Certified Public Accountants (CPA) in your area, particularly those with nonprofit audit experience.

The board then provides the CPAs on the list with the opportunity to bid on providing the annual audit. To provide consistency, the bid process could include a request for a two- to three-year audit and completion of necessary state and federal reports, such as the IRS Form 990 and Form 5500 pension report. Train your board members on how to read these legal documents, financial audits, and treasurer's reports.

The type of audit to be done will depend on the size of the nonprofit's annual budget and will be one of three primary types of audits: compilation, financial review, or audit.

ED Oversight

The final governance responsibility of board members is ED oversight. It is the board that is responsible for the hiring, supervision, and termination of the ED. Since it is not practical to have the entire board supervising the executive, it makes more sense to assign supervision responsibilities to the board chair.

The board chair or a small group of board members should conduct the ED's annual performance reviews. The review must always be based on the job description, the core competencies, and a board-approved performance review process (see **Chapter Four**).

Board's Support Responsibilities

Besides the five governance responsibilities, your board also has three support responsibilities: fundraising, public relations, and self-assessment. Although this topic is addressed in greater detail in the book, *Nonprofit Management Simplified: Programs & Fundraising*, a board member's public relation's responsibilities revolve around the fact that they own the organization, and therefore must represent it to the public in a positive way. If they cannot, then they should not be a board member. Although the spokesperson for the board is generally the board chair, every board member has a responsibility to look for opportunities to publicly support the organization.

Fundraising

If there is any perception the nonprofit does not use the proceeds from any resource development strategy in an ethical, efficient, and effective manner, the next fundraiser (regardless of the strategy used)

The Fundraising Checklist for Board Members

Board members will be more apt to understand their role in fundraising if they are presented with a checklist of items or questions for their consideration:

◆ What are the nonprofit's plans for resource development and fundraising?

◆ How do my financial contributions to the nonprofit correspond to my level of income?

◆ When have I given staff a list of potential donors, based on my community connections (individuals, corporations, etc.)?

◆ How have I assisted staff in cultivating potential donors?

◆ How do I make introductions so others can ask for the contribution?

◆ How many times in the past year have I gone with staff or key volunteers to meet with prospective donors or made visits myself?

◆ How often do I send out thank you letters to potential donors I have met with?

◆ How do I help with the annual fundraising campaign?

◆ How much money needs to be raised each year?

◆ Do I understand the nonprofit's programs well enough to ask for contributions?

◆ What are the positive outcomes of the programs?

◆ How do I serve in an advisory role to staff rather than telling them how to do their job?

will probably not succeed. And this is where the board's responsibilities come into the picture.

First, board members must periodically assess the effectiveness of all fundraising strategies (see chapter three of *Nonprofit Management Simplified: Programs and Fundraising*) but also verify the proper internal controls are being used in the processing of donations (see chapter three of *Nonprofit Management Simplified: Internal Operations*).

Second, although some nonprofit leaders will contend it's not the board's role to do fundraising, the majority of smaller nonprofits involve their board in fundraising strategies out of necessity. Without fundraising staff, such nonprofits must call upon stakeholders (e.g., board members) to assist in fundraising.

Assuming your board members have been well trained and understand thoroughly the nonprofit's vision and mission, they can play an important role in fundraising, especially in opening doors to their peers and constituents who might be potential donors. "The Fundraising Checklist for Board Members" will help them evaluate their involvement in fundraising.

Third, to assure future financial viability of the organization, it is the responsibility of board members to monitor the amount of funding coming from each source. If your nonprofit becomes too dependent on any single source, it could put your programs in jeopardy if the funding source is suddenly no longer available. A good rule of thumb is to try to not have more than 20 percent of your budget coming from any single source; that way, if the source dries up, it will not be as devastating to your nonprofit as it would be if the source is a higher percentage of your budget.

And, finally, board members must provide personal financial support to the organization. Otherwise how can they expect others to make contributions? Some nonprofits set specific giving amounts or levels for their board members.

However, I would rather have a generic policy that states, for example, "Each board member is expected to make a financial contribution to the nonprofit, commensurate with their level of income or ability."

This type of policy allows the board to choose a low-income individual to be on the board to provide valuable input on programs, especially if they have benefited themselves from the services of the nonprofit. This policy prevents the low-income board member from being forced to donate at the same level as their wealthier fellow board members.

Board Member Self-assessment

Self-assessment is a way for you and the board members to periodically review the effectiveness of the individual board members. Here are two examples of assessments that could be done on an annual basis.

Personal Participation Assessment

Knowledge

- ❑ Am I educated on the nonprofit, its history, goals, clients, staff, current situation, problems, needs, mission, vision, and values?

- ❑ Do I keep abreast of national, state, and local trends affecting the nonprofit, its stakeholders, and its mission?

- ❑ Do I educate myself on the roles and responsibilities of the board as a whole, as well as my individual board member responsibilities?

- ❑ Do I understand the legal mandates for the nonprofit?

Involvement

- ❑ Do I participate in the board's tasks?

- ❑ Am I an enthusiastic and knowledgeable voice for the nonprofit?

- ❑ Do I serve actively on at least one committee and understand how the committee relates to the board?

- ❑ Do I act as an advocate for the nonprofit and its clients?

- ❑ Do I contribute financially to the nonprofit?

- ❑ Do I participate in discussions at meetings, ask probing questions, and seek relevant answers before voting?

- ❑ Do I report to the board in written or verbal form, as appropriate?

- ❑ Do I recognize my role as a member of a team?

Time Commitment

- ❑ Do I attend board orientations, trainings, and planning sessions?

- ❑ Do I attend board meetings, committee, or general membership meetings?

- ❑ Do I complete assigned work between meetings, including preparing for meetings by reading reports and background material?

Constraints

- ❑ Do I support board decisions once they are made (even if I voted against the decision) or resign if I cannot?

- ❑ Do I avoid any possibility of conflict of interest?

- ❑ Do I understand the differences between the role of the board and staff and do not attempt to do a staff person's job or let them do mine?

Legal Governance Assessment for Boards

Rate your board of directors, not your organization, in each of the seven areas of board responsibilities on the following scale:

- ❑ "4" = We do this very, very well.

- ❑ "3" = We do this at a satisfactory level.

- ❑ "2" = We do some of this but our performance is unsatisfactory.

- ❑ "1" = We either do not do this at all or we do this very poorly.

Responsibility	Rating	How can we do this better?
Legal		
Planning		
Financial oversight and accountability		
Resource development		
Chief executive officer		
Self-assessment and board development		
Public relations		

Board and Staff Lines of Authority

One of the most frequent problems I see with nonprofits is related to the lines of authority between board members and staff.

Board members usually assume several roles within a nonprofit, and sometimes who is in charge and when can get kind of blurry. Understanding the different roles and responsibilities of board and staff can aid greatly in improving their working relationships.

Every new staff and board member's orientation should include information on the various "hats" board members can wear and when they should wear them. Clarification of this one issue can be invaluable in preventing clashes between your board members and staff. The checklist included in this chapter is a great tool to use when conflicts arise.

When a volunteer is wearing the board member "hat," policy and governance are their primary roles. In these roles, the volunteer is legally liable for the policy decisions the board makes or does not make, and you, as the ED, are the only staff person over which the board has authority. All other staff is responsible to you, not to the board.

The second "hat" a volunteer board member might wear is as a committee member. In this role, the volunteer is acting in an advisory role only. There is no line of authority over any staff. Any staff person assigned to the committee is also in an advisory role to the committee and has no authority over the committee. Although committees can develop policies, they do not make policy: That's the board's role.

Tell all of your staff involved with committees that all policy recommendations from a committee must come to you before being taken to the board. Such recommendations of policy must be evaluated based on two criteria:

◆ Does it bring harm to the organization?

◆ Does it fit with the board-approved strategic plans of the organization?

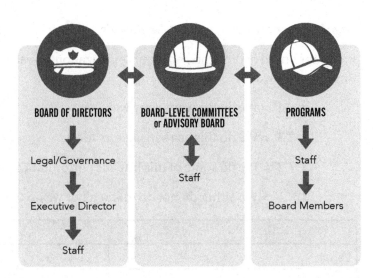

If these two criteria are not met when you evaluate a committee's recommendations, then it should not be taken to the board for a vote.

The third "hat" a volunteer board member might wear is as unpaid staff. In this role, the board member is performing a program service (e.g., serving food at the soup kitchen, fundraising, or taking tickets at a concert) and is directly responsible to the staff person who has been assigned supervisory responsibility.

Remember the story at the beginning of this chapter where the staff person was fired for not following the board member's directions? The scenario is a perfect example of what can happen when neither the ED nor the board member clearly understand their roles, responsibilities, and lines of authority. Unfortunately, the staff person was the victim of their ignorance.

Clarifying for staff and volunteers which role is appropriate for what task can be done by providing specific job descriptions for all three levels, or "hats," of responsibility. The job description must state clearly who the volunteer's supervisor is.

Once the board and staff have been trained on these lines of authority, when there are problems do not hesitate to bring out the chart and use it to gently remind folks of the proper lines of authority. The quiz in **Appendix B** is a great tool to use during a board training to help board and staff understand their roles and responsibilities.

Another hint: If it is a board member who is not following the lines of authority, it might be prudent to have the board chair remind them of the proper lines of authority. If you try to deal with it, you can get caught in the middle and it could impact your standing with the board. It might even cost you your job.

The best rule of thumb when dealing with conflicts with board members is volunteer to volunteer. In other words, even if it is the board chair you are having a conflict with, ask another board member who you trust to take the lead in discussing the issues.

Regardless of the structure the organization is using, there is often confusion on not only how many committees a board should have but also how they operate. The details of conducting effective board and committee meetings are included in **Chapter Three**. This chapter deals with committee structure only.

Types of Committees

Regardless of the size of your board, too many committees can be a nightmare for the staff who is involved with the committees, since it takes time to plan and follow-up on committee advice.

Six committees are enough for any nonprofit.

Organizational Structure Based on the Core Elements

If the committee structure is based on the six core elements of a nonprofit mentioned previously, then the number of committees will range from three to six.

Depending on the size and needs of the nonprofit, the three committees can be split into up to six committees. The key is to make sure all six of the core elements are being addressed by the board at the committee level.

Some boards will prefer to have a finance committee separate from the administration committee. No problem. Just make sure, however, the other facets of administration (risk management, equipment, facilities, and personnel management) are covered in another committee.

Too often a finance committee meets only when there is an audit, a budget, or treasurer's report to review. By combining all of the administrative responsibilities into one committee, none of the other administrative governance issues get left to chance while financial issues are still monitored.

I also suggest having a separate volunteer development committee responsible for the development of policies related to the recruitment, training, recognition, and dismissal of all volunteers: board, committee, and program.

This committee can either fulfill the traditional nominating committee responsibilities or the board could appoint a subcommittee or task force of the volunteer development committee to be responsible for board member recruitment and the selection of potential officers.

By combining the nominating committee tasks with the volunteer development committee responsibilities, emphasis is placed on the fact that board recruitment and development of all volunteers should be a year-round effort, not just in the month before the election of officers.

I find it amazing that a nonprofit with hundreds or thousands of volunteers will often not have a volunteer development staff position or a board-level committee to monitor volunteer development.

If your nonprofit has more than fifty volunteers, you need a volunteer development committee. If your nonprofit has more than one hundred volunteers, you might want to give serious consideration to hiring a staff person to be the volunteer coordinator, who would then staff the board-level volunteer development committee.

In any discussion of board-level committees, the critical question should be, "How can the board best provide oversight to all of the core elements?" And it may mean three committees or it might mean up to six committees. The number of committees and types will usually be in constant fluctuation, since the committee structure should reflect the needs of the nonprofit at any given time. Just be sure job descriptions are put together for the committees so that everyone—staff and volunteers—clearly understand the responsibilities of each committee and their lines of authority (see **Appendix C**).

Which brings up another point: The board-level committees are a great training ground for potential board members. Be sure that the chair and vice chair of every committee are board members and that every board member sits on at least one committee. Beyond those requirements, bring other community individuals on to the committees who have expertise in the responsibilities of the committee. The board leadership can then observe the non-board members on the committees to see if they would make a good board member.

Executive committees are usually composed of the officers of the nonprofit; but adding the board-level committee chairs to the executive committee improves communication and still allows the executive committee to make needed decisions between board meetings. Be cautious, however, about avoiding the potential or perception by the rest of the board that the executive committee is the "real" board and the rest of the board simply rubber stamps their decisions.

Many leaders in the nonprofit sector (especially in large nonprofits) argue that a governing board does not need committees. However, I contend that requiring all board members to be involved in at least one committee not only improves the board members knowledge of the nonprofit and the issues it is confronting, but it insures the board members own the nonprofit.

Effective Meetings

Anyone who has ever served as a volunteer has experienced the agony of long, boring committee meetings. Unless the meeting chairperson has been adequately trained, committee and board meetings can seem like a waste of time to most attendees.

If a volunteer resigns because of an ineffective meeting, it is going to be very difficult to get them to continue volunteering anywhere in the organization. Successful meetings of any type depend heavily on the skills of the facilitator or meeting chairperson. Be sure every volunteer leading a meeting has been trained in some basic meeting facilitation skills (see **Chapter Three**).

By the way, if your nonprofit has board members in a variety of locations (across the state, around the country, or around the world), you can have virtual meetings through some great computer-based programs, such as GoToMeeting.com. Just be sure the bylaws clearly state when and how such electronic meetings can occur as well as what it takes to have a quorum.

Recruitment of Board and Committee Members

The "Sample Recruitment Policies for Board Members" chart includes samples of recruitment policies and strategies for board and committee members. **Chapter Six** covers similar strategies for program volunteers.

Rewrite the sample policies to fit the needs of your nonprofit and present them to the volunteer development committee for input. The committee will then forward the final policies to the board for approval. Tools and implementation procedures can be finalized by staff at a later time as part of the development of their work plans.

Regardless of whether or not the volunteer development committee or a nominating committee handles recruitment of board members, there are some basic strategies that will help with the recruitment.

Sample Recruitment Policies for Board Members

Policy	Tools	Procedure
The board will appoint a nominating committee or task force and will bring recommendations to the board at the meeting prior to the annual meeting (per bylaws).	**Appendix A:** "Job Descriptions for Boards"	Monthly or quarterly meetings should be held to review applications, term expirations of current board members, and demographic and ethnic needs for diversity.
The nominating committee/ task force will work closely with the volunteer development committee to insure consistency in implementation of policies and procedures.	**Appendix C:** "Job Descriptions for Committees, Chairs and Vice Chairs"	Meetings will be held between the nominating committee/task force and volunteer development chairs to coordinate efforts.
A board member job description and application will be made available to all prospective board members.	**Appendix A:** "Job Description for Boards" "Board Member Application"	Completed applications should be submitted to the nominating committee/task force.
Receipt of a completed application will not be a guarantee of acceptance but is an expression of interest only.	"Board Member Application"	Applications should be screened for demographic, ethnicity, and skills; potential candidates should be interviewed; all applicants should receive a letter acknowledging receipt of the application.
The nominating committee/task force will submit board member nominees for a vote at the annual members' meeting, after board approval.	"Matrix of Board Members"	Board matrix of the entire board will be made available to show where the new board members will fill empty slots.
Board members will annually complete commitment to serve and conflict of interest statements.	"Conflict of Interest, Confidentiality and Commitment to Serve Form"	Staff will keep files on all board members and include signed copies of commitment to serve and conflict of interest statements.

Application for Board Membership

Using a board-approved form for board recruitment can really help you see if potential board members meet the criteria the board needs at any given time. This sample application should be adapted to your nonprofit's needs.

Sample Board Member Application Form

All applications for membership on the board of directors will be assessed for the board's demographic, ethnic, professional, and management needs. Receipt of a completed application will be regarded by the nonprofit as an expression of interest and not an approval by the nonprofit as a board member, or an acceptance by the potential board member as a commitment to serve on the board.

Indicate with a check mark the current status of the applicant.		Nomination has been discussed with the potential board member and they have indicated a willingness to serve if elected.
		Potential nominee has received a copy of the job description.
		Potential nominee has served on the board of a nonprofit within the past five years.
Date		
Person making nomination		
Potential board member information		
Name		
Preferred mailing address		
E-mail/website		
Daytime phone number		
Age (optional)		
Occupation		
Preferred title		
Place of employment		
Ethnicity (optional)		
Education/training		
Strengths or skills the nominee would bring to the board		

"If I am selected as a board member, I agree to adhere to all the volunteer policies and procedures, including policies related to dismissal, conflict of interest, confidentiality, and criminal background checks."

Signature:_____ Date:_____

Database

One of the most important strategies for board member recruitment is the development of a database and/or file on each board member includes at a minimum the following:

- ◆ contact information

- ◆ who recruited the individual to be on the board

- ◆ how long the individual has served and what the timeframe was, including terms of office

- ◆ offices held, committees served on, and when the individual served on those committees

- ◆ recognitions

- ◆ other community offices, positions, or recognitions received

- ◆ copies of the signed application, commitment to serve, conflict of interest, and confidentiality statements

Matrix of Board Members

To assure the board is representative of the community the nonprofit serves, it helps to develop a matrix similar to the Matrix of Board Members. This matrix is an example of the needed information for three individual board members, indicating when terms expire, demographics, etc. In this illustration, board members can serve two, three-year terms before they have to leave the board.

Sample Matrix of Board Members

Name	City	Year Elected to Board	Term	Term Expiration	Ethnicity	Gender	Region	Board Committee
Claudette Green	Austin	2009	1st	2013	Caucasian	Female	Central	Marketing
Carlos Hernandez	Round Rock	2010	1st	2014	Hispanic	Male	Central	Finance
Susie Jones	Dallas	2005	2nd	2015	African-American	Female	North	Resource Development

Recruitment Strategies

There are some specific items to take with you for the recruitment meeting with a potential board member:

- ◆ brochure or information on the nonprofit, such as the annual report

- ◆ board member job description (see **Appendix A**)

- ◆ application for board membership (see "Application for Board Membership")

- ◆ information on the slot being filled: Is the request for someone to complete a board member's term, or is the request for a first-term position?

If the volunteer development committee has done their homework, they will have a list of potential board members they would eventually like to see on the board—or the "dream team," as it is sometimes called.

Keep in mind it is not always possible to get the potential board member to say "yes" at the first ask. Maybe the person is active on another board right now but might be interested in another year or two. This is another reason why an accurate database is so important.

If you keep track of who would be willing to consider board membership in one year, two years, or more, then it will be an easy ask at the appropriate time. In the meantime, be sure the potential board member is invited to fundraising events and the annual meeting; that way they are learning a lot about the mission and will be even better prepared when they step into a board position.

Notice the sample board member application clearly states the completion of an application is no guarantee the person will be selected for board membership, but a completed application is an indication of interest.

Why is this important? Because sometimes people will indicate to you or a board member they are interested in coming on the board, but such a recommendation must be made by the board-level committee, such as a nominating committee or volunteer development committee. In other words, interest is not the same as the official ask. By using the application as the first step, it keeps you and the individual board member out of the decision-making process, especially if the nominating committee has some reasons you don't know about for not wanting the person on the board.

A new ED was wined and dined by a local real estate mogul, whom I'll call Joe. Joe introduced the executive to community leaders and educated her on critical issues within the community. She was flattered by his attention. About a month after he started squiring her around the town, Joe casually mentioned he would be interested in becoming a member of the board.

"That's great," she thought. "Joe obviously is well-known in the community. He's wealthy and seems very interested in our nonprofit."

She noticed there did not appear to be a lot of enthusiasm when she brought up his name to the nominating committee, but she did not think to ask why the apparent lack of interest in his nomination. The committee took his name to the board and he was approved.

The day after the board approved him as a member Joe walked into her office, sat down in a chair in front of her desk, and put his feet up on the desk. "I want you to know," he said, "I have been responsible for getting the EDs in two nonprofits in this community fired. And you are next."

 **stories from the real world**

As the example in the side bar illustrates, the entire recruitment and nomination process must be carefully choreographed to avoid bringing toxic individuals like Joe on to the board. The nomination process must be meticulously confidential. You, as the ED, should have input, but make sure the volunteers are the ones who make the decisions on who comes on to the board. All discussions at the meetings about potential or current board members *must* be kept confidential.

Once the nominating committee has approved an individual to be elected to the board, follow up with the new board member in person or by telephone and confirm the individual is still willing to be on the board. Once the individual says yes, have the individual sign the conflict of interest form (see "Conflict of Interest, Confidentiality and Commitment to Serve Form"), which also includes clauses related to confidentiality and the commitment to serve.

Conflict of Interest, Confidentiality, and Commitment to Serve Form

Have new and renewing board members sign this form (see opposite page).

Conflict of Interest, Confidentiality, and Commitment to Serve Form	
I do hereby declare and affirm my willingness to assume the responsibilities, as stated in the job description, and to abide by the following guidelines	
Confidentiality	To adhere to the strictest confidentiality related to any and all client or nonprofit information, unless there is illegal activity, and to submit to a criminal background check if needed
Dismissal	To adhere to the policies related to volunteer dismissal
Conflict of Interest	No member of the board or executive committee shall knowingly take any action or make any statement intended to influence the conduct of the nonprofit in such a way as to confer any financial or personal benefit on such member or his/her family or on any corporation in which he is an employee or has a significant interest as stockholder, director, or officer, with which he may serve as a director or trustee or in a professional capacity.
	In the event there comes before the board or the executive committee a matter for consideration or decision that raises a potential conflict of interest for any member of the board or executive committee, the member shall disclose the conflict of interest as soon as he becomes aware of it and the disclosure shall be recorded in the minutes of the meeting as part of the voting record.
	Any member of the board or the executive committee who is aware of a potential conflict of interest with respect to any matter coming before the board or the executive committee shall not vote in connection with the matter nor will his/her presence at the meeting (electronic or in person) be counted in determining whether a quorum exists.
These guidelines are not intended to prevent or discourage any member of the board or the executive committee from disclosing relevant information with respect to any matter to which the individual has knowledge or from answering questions or stating the individual's position with respect to any such matter.	
Acknowledgement	*I,_____, a member of the governing board of _____ (nonprofit), have read the guidelines with respect to potential conflicts of interest and the commitment to serve and agree to comply therewith. Further, I understand my continuing obligation of disclosure of potential conflict of interest should circumstances or events so warrant. I understand any expenses associated with attendance at events or meetings are my sole responsibility, unless prior approval has been given by the governing board."*

As soon as the new board member is officially elected, send out press releases to the local media announcing the new board member's election. Some nonprofits prefer to formalize the election at the annual meeting (it depends on what your bylaws say) and then a press release is sent to the various media listing all of the new board members as well as the newly elected officers.

Another strategy that can really help get new board members oriented to the organization is to pair them with a veteran board member who can respond to their questions during the first year of membership.

Recruitment Policies for Committee Volunteers

As stated previously, although the board-level committees should be chaired by a board member, bring non-board members on to the committees so the nonprofit can benefit from their expertise and experience. Examples of policies related to recruitment of committee volunteers are included in the "Sample Recruitment Policies for Committee Volunteers" table.

Although term limits aren't necessary for committee members, setting length of service terms can help to frequently bring in new members and ideas. Be sure each committee member has a copy of the committee's job description and each signs a commitment to serve, confidentiality statement (see **Chapter Six**).

Sample Recruitment Policies for Committee Volunteers

Policy	Tools	Procedure
The chair and vice chair of all board-appointed committees will be board members and will be appointed at the first board meeting of the fiscal year, per the bylaws.	**Appendix C**: "Job Descriptions for Committees, Chairs, and Vice Chairs"	All committee chairs and vice chairs will receive copies of their job descriptions.
All board members will sit on at least one board standing committee.		At the first board meeting of the fiscal year, board members will select the committee on which they will serve.
Committee work will be based on board-approved committee job descriptions.	**Appendix C**: "Job Descriptions for Committees, Chairs, and Vice Chairs"	All committee members will be given copies of the committee job descriptions.
Additional members of the committees can be community volunteers with expertise in specific areas that will assist the committees in their work.	**Appendix C**: "Job Descriptions for Committees, Chairs, and Vice Chairs"	Potential committee members who are community volunteers will be given a copy of the committee job description.
Community volunteers will complete a volunteer application prior to their acceptance as a member of a board standing committee.	**Chapter Six**	Potential committee members who are community volunteers will be given a volunteer application to complete.
Community volunteers will sign a commitment to serve and conflict of interest statement before serving on a board standing committee.	"Conflict of Interest, Confidentiality, Commitment to Serve Form for Volunteers" (**Chapter Three**)	All committee members who are community volunteers will sign a commitment to serve and a conflict of interest statement.

Board Manual

Manuals, as mentioned earlier in this chapter, should be given to all board members when they are elected to the board as one form of orientation. Some board members leave their manuals at the nonprofit's office so staff can add items to their manuals prior to the next board meeting. You, or preferably a veteran board member, can use the manual as a guide for a one-on-one orientation with new board members.

Board Training

If your board members and staff have never had training in the roles and responsibilities of board and staff, make annual training a key strategy for the orientation of new board members and staff. Training is also as a way to be constantly improving the knowledge base of both board members and staff.

If your board and staff have already been trained, adapt the training suggestions to mini-orientations for all new board members and staff. Training should be a requirement for all new board members, but ongoing training is also essential for all boards.

By the way, if you are fortunate enough to have a philanthropy center or nonprofit resource center in your community, they can be a great source of training ideas.

Another strategy for ongoing training is to include in every board meeting a ten-minute overview of a specific area of responsibility, such as the definition of policy. These types of mini-trainings keep the key board responsibilities always in front of the board.

As the board becomes more knowledgeable, ten-minute trainings at board meetings can be interspersed with information on a particular issue impacting the nonprofit's ability to function: a decrease in funding, competition, staff-turnover, legal issues, etc.

If you feel you cannot afford to hire a consultant to facilitate training for the board and staff on governance issues, ask several nonprofits to jointly pay for combined board training.

As a side note, I must add that in my more than three decades working with nonprofit boards, I can probably count on one hand the number of boards which have already had training before I was brought into the picture. And the result of this lack of training is often conflict, poor governance, and missed opportunities.

Setting up the Training

Because of the importance of board training, scheduling the training and recruiting a facilitator is your responsibility as the ED, in partnership with the board chair.

Here are some tips for setting up the training.

Facilitator

Recruit an experienced facilitator to conduct the training. Someone with nonprofit experience as either a board member or senior staff person is always a plus, since this individual will be better able to respond to questions. Check with peers to get recommendations for facilitators. A "Guidelines for Facilitators" is in **Chapter Two.**

Date

Set a date for the training at least a month in advance to allow board members and staff plenty of time to arrange their schedules so they can attend.

Time

A training held after work, with a light supper served, is a good way to get commitments so board members do not have to take time away from their weekends with their families. If a Saturday is best for everyone, schedule a two-hour training at 10 a.m. so they will still have a half day left of their Saturday. Let everyone know the session will start and end at the times indicated and then stick to the time frame! Or combine the board training with a four- to six-hour strategic planning session (see **Chapter Two**).

Location

A facility comfortable and conducive to learning might be a hotel, resort, or convention center. If the nonprofit has a large conference room, is also an option. However, board members are usually more relaxed and interactive if the training is conducted somewhere other than where board meetings are usually held.

Breaks/Meals

Depending on the time of day the training is held, provide lunch or dinner as well as some type of snack and beverages for any breaks.

Room Arrangement

How the room is arranged will depend on the facilitator's preference as well as the size of the group. Classroom style seating with tables and chairs in rows is better for a large board (more than twenty), but a U-shaped arrangement works well for a smaller group.

Handouts

It is the facilitator's choice as to which of the charts and appendixes included in this book should be incorporated into a PowerPoint presentation. Be sure enough copies are printed ahead of time, and number the pages for easy reference during the session.

Supplies

The facilitator will need the following items for the training session:

   ◆   flip charts (two) with easels

   ◆   screen

Examples of handouts to include in a board training include:

◆   agenda or copy of the PowerPoint presentation
    Hint: Do not include time slots on the agenda handed out, otherwise participants will be constantly looking at their watch to see if things are on schedule.

◆   **Appendix B:** "Roles and Responsibilities" quiz
    Hint: Do not include the answer sheet in the handouts.

◆   **Appendix A:** Board job descriptions for administrative, advisory, and governing boards

◆   internal audit and financial checklists (*Nonprofit Management Simplified: Internal Operations*, Chapter Three)

◆   financial management questions for board members (*Nonprofit Management Simplified: Internal Operations* Chapter Three)

◆   board members' self-assessments

◆   "Effective Meeting Guidelines," **Chapter Three**

◆   "Simplified Parliamentary Procedures," **Chapter Three**

◆   **Appendix D:** Job Descriptions for Committees

◆   **Appendix D:** Job Descriptions for Committee Chair/Vice Chair

Example

◆ overhead projector and screen or LCD projector with a laptop computer, plus any needed extension cords or cables

◆ marking pens

◆ name tents or badges: Write just the first names of attendees in large enough letters so the facilitator can see them from the front; name tents are good because then you can decide where people sit, mixing board members and staff.

◆ food and beverages, napkins, utensils, cups, plates, etc.

◆ attendees: Besides all board members, invite the senior staff to attend so they are trained in the same way as board members; the training also provides an opportunity for staff and board members to get better acquainted in an informal setting.

Training Agenda

The sample training agenda is for two hours. Times for each of the agenda items are approximate. Flexibility should be given to the facilitator to adjust the agenda based on the questions and needs of the participants.

Hour One: Roles & Responsibilities

◆ 15 minutes: Welcome, Introductions, and Expectations

◆ 15 minutes: Agenda and Quiz (see **Appendix B**)
Ask attendees to work in pairs to complete the quiz in ten minutes. In the last five minutes, quickly run through the answer sheet, asking them to keep track of how many answers they got right. I always like to give candy to the team with the most correct answers.

◆ 20 minutes: Responsibilities of Boards

◆ 10 minutes: Break

Hour Two: Lines of Authority and Effective Meetings

◆ 30 minutes: Lines of Authority

◆ 20 minutes: Effective Meetings (see **Chapter Three**)

◆ 10 minutes: Review of Expectations and Next Steps

Expected Outcomes of the Two-hour Board Training:

◆ Board members will understand their five key governance, four duties, and three support responsibilities.

◆ Board members will understand the lines of authority in the three volunteer positions within the nonprofit.

◆ Board members will know how to conduct effective meetings.

◆ Senior staff will understand their own lines of authority when interacting with board members serving in their three volunteer roles: governance, committee, and program.

Recognition Strategies

Most U.S. state laws define volunteers as individuals receiving $500 or fewer per year in any type of remuneration (including recognition awards), except for reimbursement of expenses. So make sure your recognition efforts do not exceed your state or country's financial requirements of volunteer remuneration.

One of the difficulties associated with providing satisfactory recognition for board members is the reasons people volunteer are very different. As a result, the types of recognition must vary. It takes some extra work to find out which recognition strategy works best for each board member, but it well worth the time to get it right.

There are board members who will be offended if you spend any money on recognition items. They would rather have the money spent for services than for plaques. Other board members like to be able to put a plaque on their office wall or to see an article in the newsletter. It is important, therefore, to know what types of recognition each volunteer will appreciate. This is just one reason why a good database for volunteers that tracks this type of information is important.

A good way to figure out what types of recognition a board member prefers is to visit them in their office. If you see a lot of plaques on the wall, then you know this is probably an acceptable recognition strategy.

You do not need to approve expenditures for tangible recognition items (e.g., gifts, plaques) as long as they are included in the board-approved budget; otherwise the expense will have to be approved by the board. Sample policies for all types of volunteer recognitions are included in **Chapter Six**.

Board Member Dismissals

Because board members are critical resources for you, providing unpaid service to keep the nonprofit's expenses low, you may be reluctant to initiate the dismissal or firing of a board member. But you also know a toxic board member can have far-reaching negative impacts on the nonprofit.

If, however, other board members make the decision on the firing or dismissal of a fellow board member, it will keep you out of the line of fire. There are three steps to take in dismissing a board member. Be as meticulous in this process as you would be in firing a staff person.

Training

Make sure when board members are recruited they understand they will be evaluated and can be dismissed if the fit is not right with the nonprofit or if they violate the bylaws regarding attendance requirements, have unstated conflict of interest issues, or if they are disruptive. This is another reason why signed forms like "Conflict of Interest, Confidentiality, and Commitment to Serve" can be of great help if and when board members need to be dismissed.

Policies and Procedures

Develop policies and procedures related to the evaluation process for board members so board members do self-assessment and the board chair can evaluate the members.

A board member told the ED he was going to get her fired. When she recovered from the shock of the statement, she called the board chair and reported the incident. "Oh I'm sure Joe didn't mean anything by it," the board chair said. "You just misunderstood."

Fuming at the board chair's failure to believe her, in confidence she mentioned the incident to another board member she trusted.

At the next board meeting, the board member in whom she had confided caught the toxic board member in a lie and confronted him at the meeting. Not long after, the board chair asked the toxic board member to resign.

 stories from the real world

The policies and procedures should state any dismissal of a board member will be done by a vote of the full board, after the board chair has met with the offending board member and discussed openly what the problem is. Check your bylaws to see what they say about resignations or dismissals of board members. If the bylaws statements are not clear, rewrite them and get board approval for the changes.

A tip based on a situation I experienced when dealing with a toxic board member: Volunteers are often reticent to fire another board member, since they have to work with the individual outside the nonprofit's walls. What I learned the hard way is it is better to allow another volunteer to confront the toxic board member. Unfortunately, sometimes boards are more willing to fire the ED than to fire a fellow board member who is disruptive.

All board member dismissals must adhere to the board-approved policies and bylaws. *Remember these are not legal opinions but suggestions and should be reviewed by an attorney familiar with nonprofits and nonprofit law.*

To Recap

◆ Board development rather than board management is a critical responsibility for every nonprofit ED.

◆ Recruitment policies and procedures are essential for good board development.

◆ Effective board development includes a variety of training strategies that encompass the five legal, four duties, and three support responsibilities of the board.

◆ All senior staff and board members should be trained in the lines of authority for the various "hats" board members wear as volunteers.

◆ Recognition strategies for board members should be based on the motivations and desires of the individual members, as stated in written policies and procedures and recorded in the volunteer database.

◆ Dismissal policies and procedures will remove the ED from conflict and allow for other board members to dismiss toxic board members.

Chapter Two

Simplified Strategic Planning

IN THIS CHAPTER

···→ The simplified planning process

···→ The agenda

···→ The follow-up

···→ Responding to change

The ED of a small nonprofit was looking for critical funding from a foundation. "You have to have a strategic plan before we will accept your application," the foundation staff person said. Having never done a strategic plan before, the ED asked some of his peers for suggestions.

"Oh, you really need to go through the college to get a good facilitator," one person told him.

"No, the best thing you can do is hire this great consultant I know," a board member told him.

The ED, with the board's approval, decided to hire the consultant, who had his doctorate in planning. The college's recommendation was for a grad student, who the executive felt was just too inexperienced.

The consultant's price was steep: $20,000. "But if this is what it takes to get this grant," the ED told the board, "then we better bite the bullet and do it." The board agreed and took funds out of the nonprofit's six-month operating reserves to pay the consultant.

After almost a year of work, the consultant handed the ED a large notebook full of information and asked for his check. The executive sat down to review the work and was appalled to discover the majority of the strategic plan was useless. Although the consultant had a lot of experience with strategic planning in the academic and for-profit sectors, he had never worked for a nonprofit, either as a staff person or during his years of consulting; and the plan showed it.

The plan contained all kinds of recommendations beyond the scope of the resources for the nonprofit, and there were huge gaps in planning around issues like board and volunteer development. Plus, many of the recommendations were now irrelevant because a lot had changed at the nonprofit since the planning process started.

The ED knew the board would find the plan to be unrealistic and unusable, so he hoped they would not ask to see it. He dutifully submitted the grant application to the foundation, along with the consultant's plan, got the grant, and then put the notebook up on a shelf where it languished for several years before the next ED tossed it out.

The Six-Hour Simplified Strategic Planning Process

(*Winner of the 2011 SEToolbelt Award for Innovation*)

Unfortunately, the example above illustrates what can happen when nonprofits try to do strategic planning, especially if the ED has never done a formalized planning process before. It also shows how important it is the nonprofit vet the consultant to make sure they have experience in working in a nonprofit.

Indicate with a checkmark the reasons why you haven't done strategic planning or, if you have, why it did not work:

- ❑ The pressures of trying to meet client needs are so great we just cannot take the time to plan.

- ❑ I have no clue where or how to start a planning process.

- ❑ We lack the funds to hire a consultant.

- ❑ We tried it, but the consultant or facilitator had no experience with nonprofits and the plan was useless.

- ❑ The process took months and by the time it was completed things had changed so much many of the recommendations were irrelevant.

- ❑ The process did not engage all of the key stakeholders, so there was no buy-in for the recommendations.

- ❑ The plan failed to incorporate all of the critical components or elements of a nonprofit, so there were big gaps in the results of the process.

- ❑ The plan did not include strategies for adapting year-round to sudden changes in the environment in which the nonprofit operates.

- ❑ We never found the time to take the results of the planning process and develop the goals into a work plan.

If you checked at least one of the statements, then you might be ready for a proven simplified strategic planning process. I am the first to admit this planning process will not meet the rigorous demands of academic strategic planning, nor will it include the potpourri of assessment information is generated during the traditional planning process. But the simplified process will jump-start any nonprofit into a planning mindset that can build a culture of long-term planning, which is a lot better than no planning.

Too often, strategic planning is seen as a long, complicated, expensive, and boring process that occurs every three to five years, with the primary goal of producing a huge document. The simplified process is just that: a one-day, simplified process that engages stakeholders in a process of evaluation and planning which never ends but allows the organization to be nimble in responding to changes around them.

For purposes of this simplified process, one-year strategic planning is the focus rather than multiyear, long-range strategic planning. Strategic planning beyond one year is increasingly difficult due to the fast-paced, ever-changing environment in which twenty-first century nonprofits operate.

One of the biggest values of a consistent strategic planning process is it can keep the organization focused on the mission. The process can also clarify what programs the nonprofit should or should not do.

I have used this simplified strategic planning method with dozens of nonprofits across the United States for more than fifteen years. The vision and mission statements many of the nonprofits developed during the simplified process are still being used. Some of the agencies now have more sophisticated assessment processes. And they are able to adapt more quickly to environmental changes than they would have been able to do using a traditional process.

Consolidating the planning process with two hours of board training (see **Chapter One**) in the morning and four hours of planning in the afternoon keeps planning costs down, since there is no expensive consultant to hire—only a facilitator. The simplified process often jump-starts annual board training and other planning strategies.

The sample agenda for the process is flexible. Time slots can be adjusted so the process fits your nonprofit's needs and your facilitator's skills.

Characteristics of the Simplified Process

The primary characteristics of the simplified process include:

◆ a four- to six-hour session with board members and senior staff (A four-hour planning session will not have as many assessments as would be possible in a six-hour session.);

◆ essential but limited assessments (depending on the length of the planning session) with more sophisticated assessments added each year;

The simplified planning process uses virtually the same terms as those in a traditional planning method ("Strategic Planning Process"). In order to make sure everyone involved in the planning is using the same definitions, the facilitator should share with the participants the terms to be used, such as:

◆ *Strategic plan*, the one-year, flexible business plan updated and built-upon every year

◆ *Vision statement*, a short, twenty-five-word-or-fewer statement of why the nonprofit exists

◆ *Mission statement*, a short, twenty-five-word-or-fewer statement of what the nonprofit does to fulfill the vision

◆ *Values*, the basic ethics and the values on which all decisions are based

◆ *Structure*, the volunteer and staff organizational structures used to carry out the strategic plan

◆ *Organizational Objectives*, the specific key goals or objectives for each of the nonprofit's divisions and on which the daily, weekly, and annual work plans are based.

The definitions of "goals" and "objectives" vary, so be sure to define them clearly for the group before you begin. The definitions I prefer are:

◆ *Goals*: the expected achievement (what)

◆ *Objectives*: the purpose of the achievement (why)

◆ *Outcomes*: the specific, measurable outcomes or results by which the fulfillment of the goals/objectives and programs will be evaluated over a period of years

◆ *Sustainability*: the strategies to allow the nonprofit to adapt to unexpected challenges that occur between the annual planning processes, including resource development for financial stability

◆ development of vision and mission statements, with no time spent on wordsmithing;

◆ a one-page report of the plan, which is easy to monitor;

◆ measureable goals and objectives;

◆ evaluation strategies for the supporting infrastructures needed to complete goals and objectives (such as budget, insurance, staffing, etc.);

◆ assignment of responsibilities to specific staff or volunteers;

◆ strategies for ongoing, year-round adaptation to changes;

◆ an adaptable process for evaluating every program or potential program;

◆ development of outcomes measurements for ongoing planning;

◆ a one-year, flexible plan updated and built-upon annually;

◆ a plan that incorporates all six of the core elements of a successful nonprofit: administration, marketing, resource development, community involvement, board and volunteer development, and programs.

Essentially, the simplified process provides the opportunity for real-time planning and response in a fast-changing world. Often traditional plans are out-of-date by the time they are published. Because this plan is only one page and focuses on the most critical issues the nonprofit needs to address in the coming year, it allows for constant shifts and adaptations of priorities as needs and funding change.

Effective strategic planning is a never-ending process with the nonprofit constantly adapting to changes in the environment, opportunities, or threats that arise. This same process is used for evaluating whether a new program is warranted or an existing one should be eliminated at any time during the year (see chapter one of *Nonprofit Management Simplified: Programs and Fundraising*).

Strategic Planning Process

The strategic planning meeting is simply an annual date for the board and key staff to get together and make sure they are all still headed in the same direction, that the vision and mission are still valid, and to add to or change goals and objectives.

The Facilitator's Responsibilities

The facilitator can make or break the planning session, primarily because the process is very fast paced and the facilitator must be able to keep the group on task. The facilitator must also be someone who has experience working for nonprofits.

A good facilitator for the strategic planning process will adhere to a set of guidelines (see the table below).

Guidelines for Facilitators

Responsibilities	Definition
Primary role	To guide the group toward completion of agreed-upon tasks
Keep good records	To assure good records are kept during the session for review at a later date; if a person is designated as the recorder, it should be explained it's the recorder's role to keep a record of the group's comments so consensus can be identified and achieved.
Focus the group	To keep the group focused; effective planning is a result of all participants being focused on the same problem, in the same way, and at the same time.
Establish agenda	To develop a clear agenda in cooperation with the ED and the board chair; an effective meeting will begin with the review of a preprinted agenda, asking the group for additions or deletions to the planned tasks. A good facilitator will also begin the session by asking for and recording each participant's expectations for the session.
Limit facilitator opinions	To not allow personal opinions to interfere with the group process; participants do 95 percent of the talking.
Establish ground rules	To establish ground rules and times at the beginning of the session; if there is a potential for discussion of a volatile topic, the meeting should begin by establishing the ground rules: e.g., no personal attacks, all opinions are to be heard, etc.
Adhere to timelines	To keep the group on the timeline; a good facilitator will watch the clock. The ED and facilitator should establish ahead of time flexible time slots for each agenda item, with the facilitator responsible for making sure all agenda items are completed in a timely manner.
Incorporate a variety of techniques	To use a variety of techniques that will insure the fullest participation of all attendees; a good facilitator will use small groups, brainstorming, the nominal group process, and other techniques to encourage involvement and consensus (see **Chapter Three**). One participant should never dominate the discussion.
Insure an interactive process	To encourage participation by using an interactive process; the facilitator adheres to the philosophy that the mind can absorb only what the posterior can endure.
Accomplish objectives	To establish objectives; the facilitator should meet with the board chair and ED prior to the first strategic-planning session to assist in the development of the agendas, timelines, process, and objectives and then assure the objectives are accomplished.

Do not hesitate to pay for a good facilitator if someone cannot be found to donate the time. If the facilitator is experienced, it will be well worth paying $200 or more per hour. Check with your local United Way, community college, or colleagues for suggestions for a facilitator.

Make sure to check the facilitator's references to verify the facilitator's abilities. Recruit a facilitator with experience working in and for nonprofits. This eliminates any need for the facilitator to take a crash course in the unique nature of the nonprofit sector.

A written contract is also necessary when working with a paid facilitator. The contract should include all the items listed in the table below.

Facilitator Contract

Item	Example
Date, time, and location	[Month Day, Year], 10 am to 6 pm, at board room
Facilitator responsibilities	◆ Provide clear copies of handouts for reprint at least three days prior to event ◆ Maintain confidentiality regarding all services, unless there is illegal activity ◆ Submit a final written report within thirty days of the planning session, including summaries of all information generated, assessment results, goals and objectives, and facilitator recommendations for implementation ◆ Review the nonprofit's bylaws (optional but really helps the facilitator to better understand how the nonprofit is structured) ◆ Cost per hour, whether the per-hour charge includes preparation and travel time; estimates for mileage, hotel, meals, and airfare reimbursement
Responsibilities of nonprofit	◆ Provide copies of requested documents and staff assistance necessary for the facilitator's preparations ◆ Provide copies of handouts for each participant ◆ Reimburse the facilitator for services at the negotiated rate per hour and determine whether mileage, meals, hotel, airfare, etc., will be paid ◆ Provide audio/visual aids, such as LCD projector, screen, easel, flip charts, masking tape, marking pens, and name tags or tents
Terms of the contract	◆ To pay a cancellation fee if the session is cancelled within seven working days of the event (e.g., $50 cancellation fee and reimbursement for any travel costs already paid by the facilitator, such as airfare) ◆ Length of time contract terms are valid; e.g., "Terms of the contract are valid for thirty days, after which it is invalid and must be renegotiated"

Besides hiring or recruiting a facilitator, you or your designee will need to complete the following tasks at least thirty days prior to the planning session:

◆ *Finalize facilitator contract.*

◆ *Decide who needs to be invited*—All board members and the senior staff are priority attendees. However, you might want to invite other stakeholders, such as major funders, other staff, clients, etc. Avoid inviting too large of a group, since they are more difficult to facilitate. Fifteen to thirty people is usually the maximum number of participants in order to allow for lots of interactive participation.

◆ *Mail or e-mail the Core Elements Assessment (see **Appendix D**) to all invited participants*—Be sure to put a deadline for folks to return the completed assessments (a minimum of two weeks before the planning meeting); the facilitator will need to have time to tally the results and then put the results into a chart.

◆ *Compile a report on the relevant information impacting the ability of the nonprofit to fulfill the mission*—this could include economic, demographic, financial, political, or social date, etc. You will present this during the assessment section of the agenda. Keep the report to no more than fifteen minutes. Use charts, graphs, and other visuals to make it understandable. Make copies of the report to hand out to participants.

◆ *Provide copies of the current vision and mission statements to the facilitator to use during the visioning process of the agenda.* The facilitator will either include it in the PowerPoint presentation of the agenda or as a handout *after* the vision and mission development process.

◆ *Arrange for food and drinks for breaks and/or lunch/dinner.*

◆ *Finalize the date and location of the planning session.*

◆ *Send out the invitations for the event*—Since there are almost always people who cannot seem to arrive on time, add a note to the invitation, "The session will begin promptly at [insert time]; so please be punctual." And then be sure you start on time!

◆ *Procure needed items:*

  ❖ name tags or tents

  ❖ a small calculator for tabulating results of assessments

  ❖ enough 1–2" colored sticky dots (like Avery labels) for each participant to have eighteen dots

  ❖ two flip-chart pads and easel stands

  ❖ masking tape (sometimes the flip-chart paper with adhesive on the back falls off the wall, so keep the masking tape handy)

  ❖ marking pens (at least two for every four to six people)

  ❖ any needed audio-visual equipment, such as an LCD or overhead projector, computer, screen, etc., plus extension cords and spare batteries or bulbs

◆ *Finalize the agenda with the facilitator and the board chair and procure necessary signatures for the contract.*

Six-hour Strategic Plan Sample Agenda

Schedule	Details	Tasks
Hour One	15 minutes	Welcome, introductions, housekeeping, and icebreaker
	10 minutes	Expectations
	5 minutes	Overview of agenda
	15 minutes	Core elements ranking assessment
	15 minutes	Review of organizational/committee structure
Hour Two	40 minutes	Development of vision and mission statements in small groups
	20 minutes	Group reports and comparison to current vision and mission statements
Break	10 minutes or 30 minute lunch, depending on time started	Snacks or lunch
Hour Three	15 minutes	Environmental assessment
	15 minutes	Core Elements Assessment results
	30 minutes	SWOT analysis
Hour Four	15 minutes	Prioritizing
	10–15 minutes	Break
	30 minutes	Goal setting
Hour Five	60 minutes	Committee reports
Hour Six	10 minutes	Summary of next steps
	20 minutes	Program analysis approach
	20 minutes	Strategic analysis approach
	10 minutes	Evaluation of planning process and workshop

Before the Planning Process

Prior to the start of the session, set up the room to accommodate everyone. Every facilitator will have a personal preference for room arrangement, but typical arrangements include:

◆ Arrange chairs and tables for the session in a U-shape, with the opening at the front (for groups of ten to fifteen).

◆ Arrange the chairs and tables in a classroom arrangement, with tables and chairs in rows and an aisle up the middle. This arrangement is best if the group is larger than fifteen people.

◆ Put a small table at the front for the facilitator to use.

◆ Place a small table in the middle of the arrangement on which to place the projector and computer.

◆ Place the screen so it is easily visible from anywhere in the room, and make sure all the equipment is in working order.

◆ Arrange water, drinks, and snacks on tables in the back of the room or in the hallway.

◆ Depending on the number of people attending, have a registration table outside the meeting room where people can register their attendance and pick up their name tags/tents.

◆ Place the handouts on the tables at each seat.

Hint: Print just the first names of attendees in large letters on the name tags so the facilitator can see them from the front of the room. If the facilitator prefers, use name tents on the tables with the tents turned so the facilitator can see them. It also helps to put the names on both sides of the tent so everyone can see the name. One of the advantages of name tents is you can decide who will sit where, mixing staff with board members, for example, rather than all the staff sitting together.

Also be sure each handout is numbered and in consecutive order. If the facilitator is using a PowerPoint, include copies of the PowerPoint in the handouts. The facilitator will not reveal the current vision and mission statements until the end of the session in hour two, so do not include it in the handouts.

The list of handouts for the session will vary, depending on the facilitator's preferences. Suggestions for handouts include (in the order in which they should be numbered):

◆ agenda (or copy of the PowerPoint pages)

◆ Core Elements Chart (see below)

◆ Core Elements Committee Structure Chart

◆ sample one-page strategic plan

◆ bar chart made ahead of time from the results of the Core Elements Assessment ("Board and Staff Comparison Core Elements Assessment")

◆ strategic planning forms (see **Appendix E**)

Core Elements Chart

Vision, Mission, and Values: *the heart of the nonprofit*

Administration & Volunteer Development: *the infrastructure of support*

Programs & Community Involvement: *the implementation strategies*

Marketing & Resource Development: *the growth, program, and capital improvement tools of the nonprofit*

Strategic Planning: *the learning culture to assure future success*

Board, Volunteers, and Staff: *the catalysts for achievement of the vision and mission*

Planning Process Agenda

The "Six-hour Strategic Plan Sample Agenda" can be adjusted to fit either a four- or six-hour session. Do not put the times on the agenda handout; otherwise participants will be watching the clock to see if the facilitator is on time.

Hour One: Introductions, Expectations, and First Assessment

The introduction to the session begins with the board chair welcoming everyone. Include in the opening instructions the following:

- ◆ location of restrooms

- ◆ location of snacks and drinks and note that participants may get up at any time for drinks

- ◆ reminder to turn off cell phones

- ◆ introduction of the facilitator with a short overview of the facilitator's résumé.

- ◆ icebreaker (optional)

Icebreaker and Expectations

The facilitator guides the rest of the introductions and conducts an icebreaker that will help participants get to know each other quickly. Whether the facilitator chooses to use an icebreaker will depend on how well participants already know each other.

A simple icebreaker can be done during the introductions. First, write on the flip chart the following questions and then go around the table asking for responses as each person gives an introduction:

- ◆ What is your name and position with the nonprofit?

- ◆ What is a little-known fact about you?

- ◆ What do you want to gain from this session?

The facilitator can control the length of the answers by telling the group all answers must be limited to no more than three sentences.

The facilitator records participants' expectations for the session on flip-chart paper and posts this sheet on the side of the room for review at the end of the session.

Overview Agenda

Review the agenda and ask if anyone has questions about the agenda items. This is where a Power Point is a big help, since the agenda can be flashed on the screen.

First Assessment: Core Elements Ranking

Put on the screen the "Core Elements Chart" and explain these will be the six core functions of the nonprofit that will provide the basis for all assessments and planning. As the facilitator reviews these core elements, ask participants to rank (see "Sample Core Elements Ranking") how well they think they are doing as a nonprofit in each element. Five means "we're the best," and one means "Help!"

The "Core Elements Chart" shows each of the core elements or primary functions of every nonprofit. Notice all the core elements are surrounded by strategic planning, since it is the never-ending cycle of assessment and evaluation that will allow the nonprofit to adapt to changing client needs and evolving community demographics.

The heart of a nonprofit is the vision, mission, and values by which it operates. For purposes of this simplified planning process, values are delegated to a separate board-level committee for development at a later date.

Once participants have completed their rankings of the nonprofit in all six of the core elements, the facilitator asks them for their rankings (5 = excellent, 1 = poor).

Sample Core Elements Ranking
(Based on eleven participants)

Administration	Resource Development	Volunteer and Board Dev.	Community Involvement	Marketing	Programs
4	2	2	2	1	5
3	3	3	2	2	4
3	2	2	3	2	5
5	2	1	3	1	5
2	1	2	2	1	4
2	1	1	1	1	3
1	1	3	4	3	5
4	2	2	2	2	5
2	2	1	2	4	4
2	2	3	1	3	4
2	1	1	3	1	3
Total: 30	19	21	25	20	47
Avg.: 2.7	1.7	1.9	2.3	1.8	4.3

Depending on the size of the group, the facilitator could ask a few people to share their rankings with the group or record all of the responses on a flip chart. A handheld calculator makes computing averages easy.

The facilitator could ask the groups to then rank the core elements with the categories with the highest ratings first. The ratings might show programs as the highest rated at 4.3. This is usually the case when this method is used. This is because the programs are the reason the nonprofit exists, and it almost always ranks the highest in this assessment. The lowest rankings might be resource development and marketing. The two are closely related because if the nonprofit does not have good marketing strategies, it will be more difficult to raise resources.

A simple core elements ranking chart can provide valuable information to the nonprofit. Although it is obviously based on perceptions, it is rare this ranking does not end up matching fairly closely the results from a more-detailed scientific assessment of each of the core elements.

This ranking starts the process of planning by a simple evaluation of the various aspects of the nonprofit and prepares the group for the more-detailed assessments in hour three.

Review Organizational or Committee Structure

The facilitator lists on flip-chart paper all of the board-level committees the nonprofit currently has. An organizational chart based on the core elements is presented (see "Core Elements Committee Structure," **Chapter One**). Participants are asked which of their current committees match the committee structure. The facilitator indicates that for purposes of this planning session, the committee structure shown in the example will be used.

If the planning group is large (more than fifteen), then the organizational chart should be changed to reflect the six core elements as six committees instead of the three as shown in the example, which is geared to a smaller group (fewer than fifteen).

The facilitator can suggest to the group that the board of directors will review the nonprofit's community structure at a separate meeting in order to decide if changes need to be made based on the planning session. Rarely should a nonprofit have more than the six board-level standing committees. More committees fragment the board's efforts and are difficult for the staff to handle.

If the core elements structure is used, traditional committees like the nominating committee are merged with the volunteer development committee, for example.

If there are more than fifteen participants in the planning session, it might be feasible for the committee structure for the planning session to be expanded to six: the administration/volunteer development committee would be divided into two committees, marketing/resource development divided into two committees, and programs/community involvement divided into two committees. Sample job descriptions for all of the committees are included in **Appendix C**.

Hour Two: Vision and Mission Statements

Once the core elements and committee structure have been discussed in the first hour, the stage is set for a more-detailed planning process and the group is ready to test their agreement on the vision and mission of the nonprofit. This section of the agenda will include the items noted below. Because there is often a lot of confusion as to the definition of vision and mission, for purposes of this process the definitions are defined here.

Vision

The vision is the why or the reason the nonprofit exists. The vision can also be stated as the "ultimate or ideal result of what the nonprofit does."

For example, a nonprofit which deals with abused children might have as their vision, "All children in our community are safe and healthy." Notice there are no action verbs in this statement. This is the ultimate goal the staff, board, and volunteers want to accomplish—not an action.

Mission

Mission statements are developed from the vision statement. It helps to remember that rarely is a single nonprofit able to accomplish a vision statement like the example. Vision statements are the ideal but are not usually totally achievable.

The mission statement will narrow the specific ways the nonprofit will work toward vision fulfillment, knowing collaboration with other nonprofits is the only way the vision could ever expect to be achieved.

The mission states how or what the nonprofit does to work toward vision achievement, such as "To educate and support services for victims of child abuse and their families."

Mission statements include action verbs like "educate" and "support." Mission statements are always more visible in marketing materials than are the vision statements. Vision statements are the passion or what drives the mission.

Slogan

A slogan is the catch phrase that embodies the vision and mission. This is the short, easy-to-understand statement of the vision/mission used in the marketing strategies.

For example, Court-Appointed Special Advocates might have as their slogan, "The House of Love."

The biggest problem with most vision and mission statements is they are way too long. None of the statements (vision or mission) should be more than twenty-five words. Any longer and volunteers and staff have difficulty remembering them. And the more words, the more difficult it is to understand the statements.

The process used in this hour strips away all the wordsmithing typical of more extensive vision and mission development processes. It forces participants to get to the heart of the issue without a lot of posturing or debating.

Usually this shortened process comes up with more useable vision and mission statements than those that are the result of days- or weeks-long processes. Slogans are three to four words developed from the vision and mission statements and are then used in marketing and branding materials.

This vision and mission development process has been used with all sizes of groups. One of the most creative results came out of a demonstration session I conducted at a national conference with about 150 people at the workshop. As a way to demonstrate how the process works and since they were all from different nonprofits, the participants were divided into groups based on the round tables where they were sitting.

In fifteen minutes, each group (table) developed vision, mission, and slogan statements for The Society to Prevent Cruelty to Slugs, a fictitious nonprofit.

One of the small groups at the national conference somehow found enough black plastic garbage bags for each in their group, cut holes in them for their heads and arms and then did a group cheer that included their vision, mission, and slogan statements. Not only was it funny and creative, but all of the participants left with a vivid understanding of the simplicity of developing the statements.

The evaluations after the workshop said it was the most fun they had in the entire conference. Why? Because they learned how to do a vision/mission process that engaged them, was fun, participatory, and fast-paced.

Example

The facilitator posts the definitions of vision, mission, and slogans and gives the group their instructions:

"You are going to be divided into small groups. You will have forty minutes to develop vision and mission statements of twenty-five words or fewer and write them on the flip-chart paper. If you have time, write a slogan based on your vision and mission statements. Appoint a recorder (someone with good handwriting who will write on the flip-chart paper) and a leader (who will make the report to the full group). Remember, you only have forty minutes, so identify key words you can all agree on and do not waste time trying to wordsmith what you come up with. Have fun with this, and be creative."

Divide participants into small groups of four to eight people. Be sure to mix up the participants so there are board members and staff in each group. Instructions and dividing into groups usually takes about ten minutes, so tell the group they have twenty minutes to finalize their statements. Most groups move their chairs into different corners of the room so other groups cannot overhear what they are saying, or if the facility is large enough, some groups can also work in other rooms.

The facilitator must be strict about the time. The facilitator can walk from group to group to monitor what they are doing and keep them on task. Advise each group when there are only five minutes left so they can wrap up what they are doing.

Note: If the planning process is four hours, reduce the vision and mission statement development time to twenty minutes.

Each group reports its results to the full group, posting its draft vision and mission statements on flip-chart paper. The facilitator helps the full group identify the key words in all of the drafts posted on the wall.

After all the reports are given and appropriate accolades are given to each group, the facilitator then puts up on the screen or on a flip-chart paper the actual vision and mission statements the nonprofit already has.

The group looks for similar words and then decides whether they think the old vision and mission statements need to be revised based on the work done in the small groups. If so, the facilitator tells the group a board-appointed committee will, at a separate meeting, review all of the recommendations from the small groups, look for consistency, and then finalize the vision and mission statements for approval by the board.

Break or Lunch

After two hours of work, the group will be ready for a ten-minute break or a thirty-minute working lunch. Be sure to allow for the breaks in the agenda by taking ten to fifteen minutes off of each of the hours. It is possible to include breaks, because many times this entire process has been used effectively in a four-hour session, rather than six hours. Six hours is plenty of time to get everything done on the agenda and still allow for breaks every one-and-a-half to two hours.

Hour Three: Assessments

During the third hour of the planning, participants learn more about the nonprofit's effectiveness in greater detail than the ratings of the core elements used in hour one:

- ◆ environmental assessment
- ◆ organizational assessment
- ◆ SWOT analysis

Depending on the available resources, the nonprofit could expand these assessments by more in-depth evaluations of every aspect of the nonprofit. Since the purpose of the six-hour strategic planning process is to reduce the amount of resources (time and people) needed to develop a strategic plan, other types of evaluations are listed below but are not necessary for this process, since each one could take months to do.

These assessments could be added for future years of planning:

- ◆ focus groups
- ◆ scientific assessments and research
- ◆ board assessment
- ◆ internal, operational assessments

◆ policies/procedures review

◆ environmental trends: social, economic, demographic, political, philanthropic

◆ program-specific assessments

◆ Total Quality Management Malcolm-Baldrige National Quality Award

◆ environmental assessment

During the first half of the one-hour assessment agenda, the ED (or designee) presents a fifteen-minute overview of the economic, demographic, financial, client, or other environmental issues impacting the nonprofit's ability to achieve their vision and mission.

Your report (preferably on a PowerPoint) will highlight challenges or threats that are significant. For example, if the nonprofit is providing services to victims of domestic violence, the report might include client statistics showing increases in the need for services because of the current economic recession and the resulting increase in violence.

The report would also include how contributions to the nonprofit have diminished because so many people are out of work. Or maybe there is a new domestic violence shelter in the community competing for funds and clients.

After your presentation, the facilitator takes a few minutes to guide the participants in brainstorming how the identified challenges will impact the nonprofit's ability to achieve their vision and mission. Record the responses on flip-chart paper and post them.

Organizational Assessment

The facilitator presents the results of the Core Elements Assessment (see **Appendix D**), which stakeholders (board and senior staff) completed in advance. Remind participants these standards are benchmarks and should not be regarded as needing a pass or fail grade. It is best if the information is presented in the format shown in the bar chart ("Board & Staff Assessment Comparison Core Elements Assessment"), which is prepared from the assessment data entered into an Excel spreadsheet.

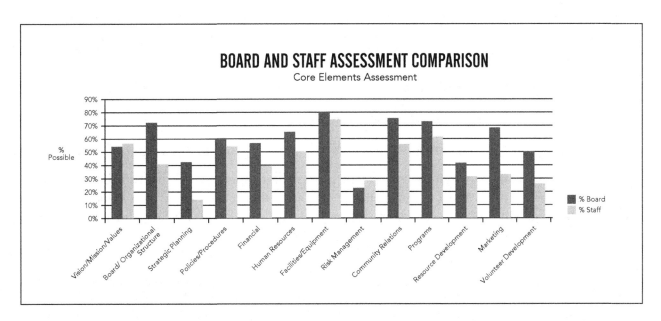

Keep the staff and board responses separate since their perceptions are always different, either because the communication between board and staff is not the best or because the staff is closer to the organization and know better what is going on.

For purposes of developing goals and objectives during the SWOT process, the group should identify the categories in the assessment where the responses show less than 50 percent checkmarks. Put those priority issues on flip charts and post on the wall.

SWOT Analysis

The final assessment is the Strengths, Weaknesses, Opportunities, and Threats (SWOT) analysis used in many traditional strategic planning processes. To prepare for this, the facilitator puts six flip-chart papers at the front on which will be recorded the participants brainstorming responses related to the six core elements of the nonprofit—one for each of the core elements.

It is helpful if each of the six papers is pre-marked as the one in the sample. Or record the responses without dividing each paper into the SWOT categories. Either process will work.

Sample SWOT Flip-chart Papers
(One page for each of the six core elements)

Strengths	Weaknesses	Opportunities	Threats
Administration			
Great staff	Not enough staff	Capacity building grant to hire staff	Funding
Good financial reports understood by board	No reserve for administrative costs or programs	Establish internal audit process	Funding
Marketing			
Been providing programs for 20 years	No marketing research	Marketing research	Funding

The facilitator guides the group in brainstorming what are the strengths, weaknesses, opportunities, and threats identified in the three assessments already done:

◆ Core Elements Ranking (hour one);

◆ Core Elements Assessment (see **Appendix D**);

◆ environmental scan or report from the ED

By reminding participants to carefully look at all of the flip-chart papers posted so far, the bar graph, the results of the Core Elements Ranking and environmental scan, the facilitator can assist in identifying all of the SWOT issues needing to be posted for prioritizing. Keep the discussions moving, and if the responses begin to dwindle, move to the next phase of the SWOT process: prioritizing.

Hour Four: Goal Setting

During the fourth hour, goal setting based on the assessments is the primary focus.

Prioritizing

Hand out the eighteen colored dots to each participant and ask the participants to write their initials on their dots so they will not forget where they placed them on the flip-chart paper.

Participants place their colored dots anywhere on the flip-chart papers that best represent the issues they think should be priorities for the strategic plan goals and objectives. It is recommended they put three dots on each of the six core elements' charts, but there is always someone who is so passionate about an issue the person wants to put more than one dot on it. Encourage all to only put one dot on an issue and only three dots on each core element page.

Break

Once participants have put all of their colored dots on the papers, they then take a ten- to fifteen-minute break. During the break, the facilitator adds up the number of colored dots on each issue and makes up six more charts, one for each core element, where the priority issues for each core element will be recorded, with the most important first. Put all of the issues in ranking order, excluding those that received no dots.

Small Group Development of Goals/Objectives

During this session, the small groups (committees) put on paper the necessary goals and objectives needed to address the priority issues identified during the assessments.

The best way to do the goal setting is to divide the participants into committees. But this time the groups are divided based on the six core elements. If there are fifteen or fewer participants in the planning session, set up three committees:

◆ committee one: marketing and resource development issues

◆ committee two: administration and volunteer development issues

◆ committee three: programs and community involvement issues.

When there are more than fifteen participants in the planning session, divide the groups by the core elements with the most issues to address.

For example, if the SWOT prioritizing shows a lot of issues in administration and resource development, then maybe five or six committees are needed:

◆ committee one: administration

◆ committee two: resource development

◆ committee three: volunteer development and community involvement (or separate this into two committees)

◆ committee four: marketing

◆ committee five: programs.

Allow participants to decide which group they want to work on but make sure there are an equal number of participants in each group and a good mixing of staff and board members. Sometimes, for example, there are a lot of participants who want to work on issues related to programs but not many for administration. It is the facilitator's job to decide what the maximum number of people will be on each committee and then to encourage people to be involved in a committee other than their first priority.

It is easier to keep track of who is on what committee if the facilitator writes the participants' names under each committee on the flip chart.

Once the committees are established, the facilitator gives the flip-chart papers prepared at the end of the last hour (the ones listing the priority issues for each core element) to the corresponding committee and they are given instructions on what to do next.

Post the committee instructions on the PowerPoint so they are easily visible or include the instructions as a handout:

❑ *Select a leader who will guide the discussion and keep the committee on task.*

❑ *Select a recorder who will complete the strategic planning forms (see **Appendix E**) as the work on each goal is completed.*

❑ *Restate each priority issue as a goal with an outcomes measurement.* For example, a priority issue for the administration committee might be: "Need to have an audit." Restated as a goal, it would be: "Goal: To prepare the financial management systems for an audit on the 2012 fiscal year finances."

❑ *For each goal, answer all of the questions in the goal setting form in **Appendix E**.* Although every participant will have at least one copy of the goal setting form in the handouts, have extra copies available in case the committees have more goals to work on than there are participants in their committee.

❑ *Identify any infrastructure issues (e.g., budget or staffing) needing to be addressed by other committees.* In the sample strategic plan, for example, the first marketing and resource development goals will require staff time and money so additional funds will need to be added to the budget and it will impact the administration committee.

❑ *Work quickly to get through as many issues as you can. The first priority should be to put each issue into a goal statement with an outcomes measurement.*

❑ *Go back and work through all the remaining questions in **Appendix E**. Any questions that do not get answered will be completed by staff as the work plan is developed for each goal.*

❑ *Be prepared to give a report to the full group that will state the goals as they are written in the example (see "Sample One-page Strategic Plan").* The facilitator needs to circulate during the committee work, responding to any questions or roadblocks keeping them from completing their instructions. Announce the time remaining at fifteen-minute intervals so they know how much time they have left to complete their work. At the end of the hour, allow a short break before reconvening the entire group.

Hour Five: Group Reports on Priority Goals and Objectives

Once the committees have completed their development of priority goals/objectives, based on the identified issues in hour three, bring them back together for their reports to the full group. The time needed for these reports will vary, depending on how many committees there are and how many issues they were working on.

Post the instructions for the reports and responses on the PowerPoint:

❑ State the issue first.

❑ Restate the issue as a goal, including the outcome measurement.

❑ Indicate any barriers or issues that will need to be addressed by other divisions of the nonprofit. (For example, if the marketing and resource development committee decides to do market research, there will be costs involved, which will impact the administration or internal management division of the nonprofit.)

❑ Give the facilitator the written reports from the committees, who will later combine all of the flip-chart papers and completed forms into a comprehensive report of the strategic planning session.

Instructions to the full group include:

❑ Listen carefully to each report and be ready to ask questions. For example:

❑ How will this goal impact our ability to raise funds?

❑ How will this goal be measured?

❑ What is the expected date of completion?

❑ How will this goal help us achieve our mission?

❑ What other areas or core elements of the nonprofit will be impacted by the goal?

If the report does not indicate what other divisions of the nonprofit will be impacted, ask them about potential impacts on legal issues, budget, facility, marketing, etc.

Remember, because this is a shortened strategic planning process, there will not be enough time to complete every analysis of every issue. The staff (or board committees) will continue the process by the development of policies and procedures related to each issue. The work being done in the session is simply a jump-start to the development of detailed work plans by the staff.

Hour Six: Establish Next Steps

The final hour of the strategic planning process is a focus on where we go from here.

Summary of Next Steps

The facilitator could recommend, for example, the completion of the following steps will be based on work done during the previous sessions:

◆ *Final report*: The facilitator, or a designated staff person, will take all of the flip-chart papers and put them into a printed, word-for-word report in the following order:

❖ list of all participants

❖ vision and mission statements as reported by each of the small groups in hour two

❖ assessments, including copies of the core elements ranking, the ED report, the bar chart from the standards assessment, and the SWOT analysis; be sure to list everything in the SWOT analysis, even the items that didn't get a vote; indicate in parenthesis how many dots each issue received

> ❖ copies of all of the committee reports (from hour five)

> ❖ a draft one-page strategic plan (see "Sample Strategic Plan"), using the goals/objectives and outcomes measurements as developed by the committees

◆ *Finalize the vision and mission statement*: The board chair can appoint a task force group of board members and staff to take the recommendations for vision and mission statements and then word smith them into statements to bring to the board for approval.

◆ *Approval of the one-page strategic plan*: Once the draft report is available, the board can review it, make any needed additions or changes, and then approve it as the "plan" for the coming year.

Program Analysis

After the analysis of the committee work is completed, the facilitator guides a discussion on how the nonprofit will respond to any critical environmental, program, staffing, budget, or demographic issues that may appear at any time during the coming year.

Appendix E includes a sample program analysis form which can be used for annual reports from every program. The same form can be used if there are any recommended changes or additions to programs during the year. Discuss with the group the items listed on the form and ask for any additions or changes to the form.

The form will then need to be approved at a board meeting and given to staff for completion when changes or additions to programs occur. Before the annual report of the nonprofit is issued, staff can complete the form as a type of mini-strategic plan for their individual programs.

Strategic Analysis Approach

Appendix E also includes a form with some of the questions a nonprofit might use during the year to respond to any unexpected issues that arise that impact the nonprofit, its programs, its ability to raise funds, etc. The facilitator can guide a discussion of whether the form needs to be changed. The final form for strategic analysis of issues will need to be approved by the board.

Evaluation of Planning Process and Workshop

The facilitator refers back to the expectations flip-chart paper developed during hour one. The group responds to the question: "Which of the expectations listed were met and which were not?" For any not met, the board chair or the ED can respond as to how and when the issue might be addressed.

For example, someone might have indicated they wanted to learn more about the role of a board member. Since the session was about strategic planning, not board development, the ED or board chair could indicate when the next board training session will be held.

Wrap up by Board Chair

As the last thing on the agenda, the board chair does the following:

◆ thanks the facilitator and the participants for their time

◆ indicates there will be another strategic planning session next year

◆ asks everyone to complete the evaluation form (**Appendix E**) and to turn it in before they leave

Final Thoughts

Here are some final comments about implementation of any strategic planning process.

Follow-up must be a priority. If there is no assignment of responsibility to build on the work of the planning session and to develop work plans for staff and volunteers, for example, people will be hesitant to be involved in future planning.

Use a computerized software system, such as WePlanWell or Envisio, to keep track of outcomes measurements and goal achievement.

Sample Strategic Plan		
Community Child Abuse Center *Vision:* All children in our community are safe from sexual abuse. *Mission:* To educate the community, develop effective programs, and support the victims of child abuse. *Values:* Equal treatment for all; children should be safe; voluntarism is the best way to initiate change, etc. *Slogan:* An open door to love		
Marketing and Resource Development	**Programs and Community Involvement**	**Administration and Volunteer Development**
A three-year marketing plan will be developed that will increase brand identity by 30 percent.	A community-wide collaboration of agencies addressing similar issues will be convened within one year.	An accounting firm will be recruited to volunteer to handle the financial books for the first year of operation.
A three-year research plan will be developed that will allow for ongoing responses by stakeholders and the general public to brand awareness strategies.	A community-wide needs and resource assessment will be developed, with the collaboration partners as stakeholders.	A paid ED will be hired within two years.
Within one year, all material used by the nonprofit will reflect brand identity strategies and logo.	The nonprofit will be a catalyst for the development of a community-wide plan for reducing the number of child abuse victims.	A system of internal financial controls will be developed and implemented for testing within one year.
A three-year fundraising plan will be developed, which will increase financial resources by 30 percent per year.	A written plan for each program will be submitted to the board within the next three months.	The board will be expanded to twelve members by the end of the year.
The number of grants written will increase 25 percent per year.	Each program will develop three- to five-year plans for implementation of outcome measurement strategies.	A detailed policies and procedures manual will be developed within two years.
A planned giving program will be established, with the first $100,000 bequest within two years.	Criminal background checks will be done on all staff and volunteers before they are hired or become involved with the nonprofit.	Board-level committees will be appointed to address administration, board/volunteer development, programs, community involvement, marketing, and resource development.

To Recap

A simplified strategic planning process will include the following components:

◆ A fast-paced, engaging, and facilitated process that includes board members and senior staff

◆ A variety of assessments to identify key issues confronting the nonprofit

◆ A review or development of concise and useable vision and mission statements

◆ Prioritized goals and objectives for all six of the core elements of a successful nonprofit

◆ Preliminary action steps for implementation of goals and objectives

◆ A one-page strategic plan on which work plans of staff and volunteers are based

◆ Strategies for analysis of unexpected issues or changes that impact the nonprofit and the programs in between annual planning sessions

Chapter Three

Effective Meetings

IN THIS CHAPTER

···→ Rationale for a one-hour meeting

···→ Nine principles of effective meetings

···→ Developing an agenda

···→ Conducting the meeting

···→ Training the meeting chairs and vice chairs

One of the most frustrating times for me at board meetings was when the board chair lost control of the meeting, with everyone stating an opinion but accomplishing little. I'm sure my fidgeting did not help keep the group on track.

I decided, "The mind can absorb only what the posterior can endure" should be the motto of everyone who leads a meeting.

Unfortunately, three- to four-hour board or committee meetings are not unheard of. Volunteers sometimes leave these long meetings frustrated because little was accomplished. So why are meetings with your volunteers often so long and unproductive?

There are at least eight reasons: The person facilitating the meeting has no clue how to conduct a meeting. There is no written agenda. If there is a written agenda, it does not have time allotments on it. Participants in the meeting have never been trained on how a meeting is supposed to be conducted. The person in the leadership position is always the same one, so things continue to be done the way they have always been done: long and boring meetings. No one is keeping an eye on the time. Participants waste time discussing items or issues that are not their responsibility or are not on the agenda. There are no minutes kept on the meeting. No parliamentary procedures are established ahead of time.

Changing the structure and effectiveness of a nonprofit's meetings will not happen overnight. But it is possible to make one-hour, effective meetings the norm rather than the exception if you follow a few basic principles.

If the meeting principles are followed, eventually the volunteers will enthusiastically embrace the idea of one-hour meetings.

There are times the scope of a meeting may necessitate a longer meeting, but if it is going to be more than two hours, suggest to the chairperson the meeting be adjourned, with a follow-up meeting at a later date. Before the next meeting, conduct any research need for a questioned agenda item, schedule another meeting, and then finish the discussion and make decisions. The goal should always be a one-hour meeting.

The key components of effective one-hour meetings are:

- ◆ adequate preparation

- ◆ written agendas

- ◆ trained meeting facilitators

- ◆ concise minutes

- ◆ productive follow-through

Preparing for the Meeting

Preparing for a meeting should be the joint responsibility of the designated staff (usually you as the ED) and the volunteer leader of the meeting.

Determine what type of meeting it is: board meeting, committee meeting, task force, advisory board, etc. The type of meeting will impact how the meeting is conducted. For example, a board meeting's focus must be on governance and policy issues, not details.

Committee, advisory boards, and task force meetings are where policies might be developed for board review, where advice is given to staff on specific procedures, or where recommendations are given to staff for implementing board-approved policies and the strategic plan.

However, board, committee, and task force meetings should never be used as opportunities for volunteers to tell staff how to do their job.

Additional information on the roles, responsibilities, and lines of authority for volunteers and staff can be found in **Chapter One**.

Board meetings often turn into committee meetings when details and procedures are discussed. Even if the nonprofit has no paid staff and functions as an administrative board, board meetings should only focus on governance, such as legal issues, policies, finances, and strategic planning.

Discussion of the details of procedures, development of policies, or advice to staff should be relegated to separate committee meetings. The board discusses and votes only on governance issues like the financial report or on specific policies.

Nine Principles for Effective Meetings

Nine basic principles for meeting preparation apply to any meeting, not just to a board meeting.

Principle One

Every committee and board should have a job description.

Job descriptions provide the parameters around which every meeting revolves. If there is no job description, then participants will have a tendency to go off on tangents and get into discussions related to another committee's responsibilities, or they will start meddling in staff responsibilities. Sample board and committee job descriptions are included in **Appendix C**.

Principle Two

Do not have a board meeting unless there are at least three items on which to vote.

If volunteers and staff know specific decisions will be made at the meeting, they are more apt to attend and participate. Fewer people will attend meetings if the purpose of the meeting is discussion and not decision-making. The voting process causes participants to feel a sense of accomplishment.

Even a committee meeting should focus on decision-making about what needs to go to the board or what issues need more work before the next meeting. Voting on items not only provides a sense of accomplishment but it also forces the group to act, not just talk.

Principle Three

Always have a printed agenda with time slots for each item.

The agenda provides the parameters around which the meeting revolves.

Principle Four

Identify who should attend and why.

If it is a board meeting, obviously the board members will be invited, but are there other people who need to attend to provide clarification or input on an issue or policy the board will be discussing? Decide if outsiders need to stay for the whole meeting or just until their participation is completed. Which staff should attend and why?

If it is a committee meeting, will participants have all the information they need for their discussions, or are there community members or staff need to attend who have the knowledge the committee needs for their discussion?

Principle Five

Train the meeting chairperson, staff, and participants.

The level of knowledge and the abilities of the person leading the meeting are critical to the meeting's success. If the leader of the meeting, or facilitator, is more interested in talking (or rambling) than accomplishing something, then the leader should either not be leading the meeting or should be trained in effective meeting facilitation.

Just because someone is a corporation executive, for example, is no guarantee the individual knows how to run effective meetings. And if your senior staff is trained on how to conduct effective meetings, they will be better able to provide support to the volunteers leading the meetings.

Principle Six

Always prepare logistically for a meeting.

❑ Make sure the room where the meeting will be held is conducive to the committee work. The room should be neither too hot nor too cold.

❑ Eliminate as many distractions as possible. A messy meeting room, for example, with stacked chairs or papers lying around will not set a good tone for a meeting. Meeting rooms with windows that look out on a busy street should have curtains or blinds on them to avoid distractions during the meeting.

❑ Determine if any audio visuals will be needed: overhead projector, LCD projector and computer, easels, pencils, etc.

❑ Provide water and/or coffee and, depending on the time of the meeting, a snack or meal.

❑ Name tags or name tents are necessary if any of the participants are new to the group.

❑ Have extra copies of the agenda or previous meeting minutes for participants who fail to bring copies with them.

Principle Seven

Every meeting requires concise minutes.

Whoever is in charge of the meeting—volunteer or staff—must make sure that the minutes of the meeting are taken by a designated volunteer or staff person. Minutes should never include details on any discussion or list who said what.

Since their names should be listed at the beginning of the minutes as "present," there is no need to include their names as voting for a motion. Also include at the beginning of the minutes the names of members who are absent from the meeting.

The names of individuals should only be included in the body of the minutes if they vote "nay" on a motion or if they are designated for a specific responsibility.

By including the names of the people with a nay vote, the individual is protected in the event a legal issue arises later. If there are no nay votes, the assumption is everyone present voted in favor of the motion.

A one-sentence description of any discussion is usually sufficient. For example: "The annual fundraiser was discussed," rather than, "Susie Jones stated she feels the annual fundraiser should be held in March instead of January. Joe Smith disagreed, but Sam felt September would be a better time."

Motions and the results of the vote are to be included in the minutes. A simple code to use in the minutes after the statement of the motion is "M/S/P" or "motion made, seconded, passed." At the beginning or end of the minutes, explain what the code means with an asterisk. If the code is used after each motion, then there is no need to write it out after each motion. If there are nay votes, the code used would be "M/S/P, with Joe Smith voting nay."

Minutes will rarely be more than one or two pages if the strategies above are implemented.

Principle Eight

Follow through on decisions made at the meeting.

Be sure individuals responsible for following up on decisions made at the meeting are identified, with their names included in the minutes. If, however, multiple individuals are responsible (e.g., resource development committee or the finance division), list only the name of the committee or staff division responsible.

The designated staff person for the meeting, a key volunteer, or the ED is responsible for making sure the right people are reminded or notified in a timely manner of their responsibilities.

Principle Nine

Meetings goals should be connected to the strategic plan.

A strategic plan (see **Chapter Two**) will have goals for every facet of the nonprofit. This means every meeting, whether it is a board or committee meeting, should include updates on the progress toward completion of at least one strategic planning goal.

Develop a Written Agenda

The first step in developing a good, written agenda is to review the minutes of the last meeting for items that must be reported on or brought forward to the next meeting. The review will identify the following:

- items for the consent agenda
- items tabled at the last meeting for discussion at this meeting (old business)
- regular committee reports (new business)
- updates on strategic plan goal(s)
- policies for discussion or referral (new business)

A consent agenda or consent calendar refers to a section at the beginning of the agenda where routine items and resolutions can be grouped. Items on the consent agent generally do not need discussion, although a board or committee member can ask for an item to be removed from the consent agenda and placed under old or new business.

All of the items in the consent agenda are voted on at one time, with one motion, without any additional explanations or comments. Because no questions or comments on these items are allowed during the meeting, this procedure saves time. Consent agendas only work, however, if participants read the supporting documents prior to showing up for the meeting.

Items in a consent agenda might include:

- minutes
- staff reports
- routine correspondence
- notification of changes in a procedure
- routine revisions of a policy (e.g., changes in dates or dollar amounts due to changes in laws)
- address changes
- standard contracts used regularly

◆ signatory authority for a bank account

◆ notification of receipt of a grant

◆ ratification of the executive committee (EC) minutes, since decisions made by the EC should be ratified by the board at their next meeting

Once the items to include on the entire agenda have been identified, the staff draft and the committee or board chair approve the agenda.

Sample Agenda—Board of Directors Meeting
[Date, Time, and Place]

Item	Time	Responsibility of	Supporting Documents (page #)
Welcome/ introductions	Noon to 12:05p.m.	Board chairperson	none
Approval of agenda	12:06 p.m. to 12:08p.m.	Board chairperson	Agenda (#1)
Approval of consent agenda	12:09 p.m. to 12:10 p.m.	Board chairperson	Minutes of the last meeting (#2); ED report (#3–4); Executive Committee minutes (#5); Signatory changes on bank account (#6); Committee reports (#7–12).
October financial report	12:11 p.m. to 12:15 p.m.	Finance Committee chairperson	Financial report (#13-16))
Old Business: 1. Resource Dev. Committee 2. Marketing Committee 3. Administration Committee	12:16 p.m. to 12:46 p.m.	1. Resource development committee chairperson 2. Marketing committee chairperson 3. Administration committee chairperson	1. Final report on fundraiser (#17) 2. Approval of revised marketing plan for 2013 (#18–19); 3. Approval of revised policy related to Directors and Officers (D&O) insurance (#20)
New Business: 1. Update on strategic plan goals for third quarter 2. CPA contract for 20xx audit	12:46 p.m. to 12:56 p.m.	1. ED 2. Treasurer	1. Strategic plan goals' chart (#21) 2. CPA contract (#22–25)
Next meeting date	12:57 p.m. to 1 p.m.	Board chairperson	

Conduct Training on Effective Meetings

If your nonprofit has a culture of ongoing learning, staff and volunteers will be better prepared to accomplish designated tasks, such as meeting facilitation. Make training in meeting facilitation a requirement for all new board members, officers, and staff, but train the participants, too.

It's okay to take time at the first meeting of a committee, for example, to tell the group concerted efforts will be made to keep meetings to one hour but in order to do so, the leadership and the participants will be trained in how to conduct an effective meeting.

Effective Meeting Guidelines

Effective meetings don't just happen. Meetings that accomplish something always adhere to specific guidelines.

Effective Meeting Guidelines

Guideline	Description
Agendas are specific and adhere to timelines.	Agendas are based on reports and updates on items discussed at the last meeting. They focus for board meetings is on policy and governance issues rather than committee reports. They are based on timelines and objectives of committee (job descriptions), board and/or strategic plan goals, which are updated annually.
Meetings should be one or two hours and are held in a room with limited distractions and comfortable chairs.	The mind can absorb only what the posterior can endure, so keep meetings short and on task. Hold meetings in a location with the least distractions.
New business is added only with consensus.	Items not on printed agenda tabled until next meeting, unless group agrees to include them at the current meeting as new business.
Have enough items for a vote.	Do not have a meeting unless there are at least three items for a vote.
Include a financial report.	If you are operating on a budget, each meeting should include a financial report.
Take minutes but include only items for a vote, not discussion.	Minutes of the last meeting should be approved at the next meeting. Minutes should not include details of discussions but only items on which a vote was taken.
Embrace conflict.	Conflict in a meeting is not necessarily bad but can be the catalyst for change and progress.
Train meeting chairpersons and members.	A study of group process, conflict management, and facilitating are helpful for any meeting chairperson and committee member.
Deal with disruptions and absent members.	Committee members who consistently disrupt meetings or attend infrequently should be met with in private and gently but clearly asked for the rationale for their behavior. If that does not work, it may be necessary, in extreme circumstances, for the group to bring pressure to bear on the individual, either by direct confrontation or by requesting their resignation.
Recognize volunteer involvement.	Develop recognition strategies for all meeting participants.

After each meeting, the facilitator or chairperson should run through the "Meeting Checklist for Facilitators or Committee Chairpersons" (see **Appendix F**) to see if there need to be any changes in the next meeting's format:

There will be some volunteers who think they do not need the training, but if the nonprofit makes training a requirement, then everyone will know how the meeting should be run and can hold each other accountable. Trainings can also be conducted by experienced, knowledgeable volunteers, but be sure they use an approved agenda for the training. Effective meeting facilitation can also be incorporated into the regular board training, rather than as a separate training.

By the way, I learned the hard way (too many long meetings) that I could help keep the board chair on track and on time if I sat next to the chairperson. If the meeting was getting off track, I would either slip a note to the chair or whisper a suggestion.

You can communicate the importance of effective meetings in such a way that all participants will work toward keeping the meeting to one hour. Each participant then takes ownership for a smooth-running meeting. Include in the training the following items:

- ◆ overview of the job description (see **Appendixes A** and **C**);

- ◆ "Effective Meeting Guidelines"

- ◆ "Facilitator Guidelines" (see **Chapter Two**)

- ◆ "Simplified Parliamentary Procedure"

Write Concise Minutes of Meetings

The staff person or volunteer designated to take minutes at the meeting should also receive training on the proper way to take minutes. **Appendix G** includes a sample of board meeting minutes, based on the sample agenda earlier in this chapter.

Meetings are always more effective when some type of formalized procedures are adopted. Although *Robert's Rules of Order* is the most complete book of meeting rules and procedures, for most meetings implementation of all of the rules would require recruitment of a parliamentarian or sergeant at arms. Make it easy on yourself and your volunteers by adopting an easy to use set of procedures, as outlined in "Parliamentary Procedure (Simplified)."

Parliamentary Procedure (Simplified)

Kind of Motion	Object of Motion	Effect of Motion
"Table"	Clear the floor for more urgent business	Delays action
"Question"	Secure immediate vote on pending motion	Ends debate
"Limit/extend time"	Provides more/less time for discussion	Shortens/lengthens discussion for debate
"Postpone definitely (to a certain time)"	Gives more time for informal discussion and for securing followers/support	Delays action

Kind of Motion	Object of Motion	Effect of Motion
"Commit/refer" (to a committee)	Enables more careful consideration to be given before a vote	Delays action
"Amend"	Improves the motion	Change the original motion
"Postpone indefinitely"	Prevents a vote on the question	Suppress the question
"Point of order"	Calls attention to violation of rules	Maintains parliamentary procedures
"Appeal the decision of the chair"	Helps determine the group's attitude on the ruling by the chair	Secures ruling by the group rather than by the chairperson
"Move"	Brings an item to a vote	Stops discussion temporarily; requires a second for action by the group
"Second"	Moves motion to action	Forces group to take specific action
"Discussion"	Calls for a discussion on the motion	Gives chance for addition discussion on seconded motion
"Say 'aye/nay'"	Call for the vote	Ends discussion and asks for group consensus

To Recap

◆ Make an effort to keep meetings to one hour in length.

◆ Be sure the room is prepared and essential handouts are ready before the meeting.

◆ Follow the nine principles of effective meetings.

◆ Always have a written agenda.

◆ Train meeting leaders in how to conduct effective meetings.

◆ Ensure minutes of the meeting are concise and include primarily the motions made at the meeting.

Chapter Four

ED Performance Reviews

IN THIS CHAPTER

···→ Rationale for an ED performance review

···→ Board-approved policies for the ED performance review

···→ ED self-evaluation

···→ Performance review meeting with the board chair

···→ Salary and benefits tied to the performance review

When the new ED asked when to expect a first performance review, the board chair replied, "We pay you so little. How can we criticize what you are doing? We're just thankful you're here!"

The ED finally convinced the board an annual performance review was wanted and needed. The ED wasn't sure how to go about establishing a review process since the ED was new to the nonprofit sector. So, the new board chair put together a package of questions and then asked the EC to evaluate the ED's performance.

Problems arose, however, when the board chair failed to do a summary of the evaluations, and the review was not tied to the job description. Board member responses were sometimes nebulous and often confusing.

One board member, for example, said, "The ED spends entirely too much time in the office." Another board member said, "The ED does not spend enough time in the office." Plus, some of the comments were based on apparent personal slights and differences of opinion on the methods the executive used, rather than on the results.

Obviously the review was useless with that kind of conflicting information.

Rationale for an ED Performance Review

You may be hesitant to request your board complete a review of your performance for one or all of the following reasons:

◆ "I've never had a performance review as an ED."

◆ "I do not know how to motivate my board to do my review."

◆ "The board has no idea what I do every day, so how can they possibly do a review?"

◆ "I have no clue how an ED review should be done."

Annual ED performance reviews are essential. How else are you going to know how the board views your performance? Plus, reviews provide opportunities for you to develop personal and professional goals related to the overall strategic plan of the nonprofit.

The board that reviews the ED annually will find they have a better understanding of the issues and pressures confronting you and will then be able to provide guidance for addressing specific problems.

Reviews tied to the achievement of strategic goals for the nonprofit will also provide valuable insight to the board on overall organizational efforts toward fulfillment of the mission.

A good review process includes analysis of management effectiveness, core competencies, and goal achievement and is tied directly to the job description. The recommended process (see **Appendix F**) eliminates subjective issues and focuses instead on measureable goals and objectives.

The actual review will take about an hour for you to complete the self-evaluation and another hour for your supervisor (usually the chair of the board) to do their review, including a meeting with you to review the recommendations.

Board Approval of Performance Review Policies

A critical component of the development of the performance review process is the board approval of policies related to the review. Once the policies have been approved, the supporting documents—such as the ED job description, core competencies, and performance review—can be finalized.

One of the key policies the board must develop is related to how the board decides when and how much the ED should receive in salary increases. Such salary reviews *must* be based on the review, not on subjective issues like how much board members like the executive.

Sample Executive Director Performance Review Policies

Policy	Timeline	Responsibility of
The ED's supervisor is the board chair, per the bylaws.	During the board chair's term of office	Board chair
The ED will be evaluated annually by the board chair or designees.	Within thirty days of the anniversary date of employment	Board Chair
The ED review will be based solely on the board-approved core competencies and job description.	Plan and process will be reviewed at least three months prior to scheduled review	Members of the board's administration or EC

Policy	Timeline	Responsibility of
The senior staff will evaluate the ED's supervisory and communication skills.	One month before the ED review is to be completed	Board chair
The board members will evaluate only the ED's leadership and communication skills.	One month before the ED review is to be completed	Board chair
The board chair will prepare a written summary of the senior staff, board member, and board chair evaluations to give to the ED during the review meeting.	One week before the executive review meeting with board chair	Board chair
The ED will prepare a detailed overview of accomplishments during the year, based on the core competencies, and will do a self-evaluation using the same form as the board chair uses.	One week before the ED review meeting with the board chair	ED
The ED will prepare a written response to the evaluations; it and the board chair's review will be filed in the director's confidential personnel file, along with all of the review documents.	Two weeks after the review meeting with the board chair	ED
The ED's review is confidential and will be available only to the director and the EC.	Within two weeks of the ED review meeting with the board chair	Board chair
The board chair will present a confidential report of the results of the review to the EC in a closed-door session.	Within one month of the completion of the review	Board chair
The salary review will be based on the performance review.	Within one month of the completion of the review	Board chair

Steps for Developing an ED Review Process

To develop and implement the ED performance review, there are five steps the board must take.

Step 1: Develop a Core Competencies Document

Ask the board chair to appoint one or two board members to help you to develop a list of core competencies critical for you to have in order to be able to fulfill your duties.

The sample "Core Competencies of an ED" (see **Appendix H**) is based on decades of my own experiences. Add items or subtract any irrelevant items that apply specifically to your nonprofit's management. Get board approval for the core competencies document.

Step 2: Review the ED Job Description

Make sure your job description matches the core competencies and reflects your current duties as ED. Take the revised job description (see **Appendix I**) to the board for approval.

Step 3: Determine the Review Process

Have the board approve policies related to the review process so the same process will be used every year for your review, such as the example in **Appendix J**. Remember, your performance reviews should be different than the process used for other staff (see **Chapter Six**). You are the only staff person directly accountable to the board, an element that is not an issue in the reviews of other staff.

Determine if you want your senior staff to also do a review of your supervisory skills. While it initially might not sound like a good idea, providing your staff with the opportunity to provide feedback on your supervision skills can help you to identify areas needing improvement. Just be sure their review is done in such a way that maintains their confidentiality in order to avoid any appearance of potential retaliation for saying negative things about their boss.

Once the board has determined the process to be used, all of the documents (job description, core competencies and performance review) should be examined by an attorney familiar with state and federal labor laws in order to make sure they are in compliance.

Step 4: The Review

Using the board-approved core competencies (see **Appendix H**), job description (see **Appendix I**), and the review document (see **Appendix J**), the ED does a self-evaluation. Once you have completed your personal review, give it to the board chair (or whoever is doing the review) a couple of weeks prior to the sit-down review.

Another good item to include with the self-evaluation is a detailed listing of your accomplishments during the year. This is especially important because your board members rarely see you in action from day to day, so how else will they know how you spend your time?

It is easy to complete the self-evaluation if you keep a journal of each day's activities, including the amount of time taken for each item listed. This can be done on the computer and then easily consolidated and printed out for the review.

The ED Journal

Date	Description	Time (hrs)	Organizational Objective or Core Competency	Core Element
9/7	Staff meeting	1.5	Provides effective staff leadership	Administration
	Board meeting preparation	1	Provides leadership	Administration
	Phone calls to potential board members	1	Relationship builder	Board/volunteer development
	Attended Rotary meeting	1.5	Skilled at community building and collaboration	Community involvement
	Reviewed donor database and prioritized potential leadership givers for contact by volunteers	2	Skilled at resource development	Resource development
	Met with staff accountant regarding first audit; did internal audit; worked on financial policies to take to the Finance Committee	2	Goal 1: Administration division CPA to complete an audit Goal 2: Meet standards of accounting for nonprofits	Administration

Organize the journal by date, by categories based on the strategic plan goals, by the core competencies, or by the core elements. By keeping a detailed record on an Excel spreadsheet, for example, it is easy to show how much time is being spent on what. The time journal (see **Chapter Five**) can also be used for accounting purposes to allocate your salary by program or administration costs, based on the amount of time you spent in each area.

The journal makes it is easy to organize goal achievements and tasks by strategic goals and/or core competencies. The total number of hours you worked on each organizational objective or core competency can be shown on a summary sheet as an attachment to the review.

Take the detailed journal with you to the review in case the board chair wants to see it. A well-documented journal shows the chair of the board exactly how you are spending your time each day. Typical journal entries for one day might look like "The ED Journal" chart (see opposite page).

The face-to-face meeting with the board chair for the formal performance review provides both of you with an opportunity to objectively analyze performance areas, based on the input of the nonprofit's key volunteer and your supervisor. Although you may disagree with the board chair's review, the self-review and documentation on what was accomplished can be used to balance what might be a negative review.

Your attitude toward the review can make a big difference in how the meeting with the board chair goes. If you see the review as an opportunity, rather than something to be dreaded, the session will go more smoothly.

However, one of the aspects of nonprofit management sometimes difficult for any ED is building a positive relationship with the board chair. Every board chair is different and some are easier to get along with than others.

A problem you might face is when the board chair is too dictatorial and tries to tell you how to do your job. This can make for an uncomfortable and difficult performance review. Sometimes board chairs can

A veteran nonprofit ED was asked to serve as asked to serve as the Chief Executive Officer (CEO) to help in the merger of two nonprofits. It wasn't until the CEO was on board that he realized there were some significant issues the newly merged board had failed to tell him about.

◆ One of the nonprofits in the merger had been staffed for several years by an ED who had been borrowing from one federal grant to pay the expenses of another federal grant—an illegal activity. In spite of this, the board asked the CEO to put the ED on staff as a vice president (VP) to avoid potential problems because the VP represented a minority group. The VP had also applied for the CEO position of the merged nonprofit and was resentful of the new CEO.

◆ The ED of one of the nonprofits had retired with a huge pension, which the other staff deeply resented.

◆ Before the CEO was hired, and based on the recommendation of the long-time auditor, the board approved the purchase of an extremely complicated accounting system but did not train the existing bookkeeping staff on how to use the software. And they did not bother to tell the CEO the staff was not qualified to use the software.

These were just a few of the problems confronting the new CEO. When it came time for his performance review at the end of the first year, the CEO was frustrated to discover the board was using the difficulties associated with these issues as negatives in the CEO's performance, even though it was the board that had caused the problems. Although the CEO worked hard to correct the problems, it was clear from the comments in the performance review that the CEO was going to take the hit for the mistakes the board had made.

Example

Salary and benefits surveys conducted by some of the organizations listed here can help the nonprofit determine what the salary and wage ranges should be for employees. However, sometimes just checking with other nonprofits in your area as to what their salaries and benefits are can work just as well. Other potential resources include:

◆ Alliance for Nonprofit Management, a professional association for nonprofit executives interested in "raising the bar on quality;" 1899 L Street NW, Sixth Floor, Washington, DC, 20036, 202-955-8406, 202-955-8419 (fax), alliance @allianceonling.org, *allianceonline.org*

◆ *Nonprofit Digest*, the journal of innovation for nonprofit leaders and scholars, published by The Global Institute for Nonprofit Leadership, in cooperation with Civicus Consulting

◆ *The Chronicle of Philanthropy*, a weekly newspaper format with the latest news of interest to nonprofits, including annual surveys on salaries and benefits for nonprofits, display@philanthropy.com, *philanthropy.com*

◆ *The Nonprofit Times*, magazine format, *nptimes.com*

practical tip

use the review as another opportunity to dictate what should or should not be done. Unfortunately, this often occurs when the ED is female and the board chair is male.

Hopefully the nonprofit has term limits for board officers, which prevents such a board chair from being in the position for more than one year. It is comforting to know the situation will get better after a year.

Honesty is always best, but communicating with this type of board member can be uncomfortable. If the situation gets too bad, consider talking confidentially about the situation with another board member whom you trust and ask the individual for advice. You might also want to ask the board chair to have the trusted board member to participate in your review.

Or if there is a lot of animosity between you and the board chair, request the review be done by two or three members of the EC. Or request another board member be present for the review with the board chair.

The best way to handle a difficult performance review is to make sure everything that was done the previous year is documented and included in the personnel file. You have the legal right in most states to add a letter to the personnel file that is a rebuttal to the negatives in a performance review.

Encourage the board chair to focus on the core competencies and the review categories and avoid getting into other issues that are not relevant to the review.

Step 6: Report to the Board

For confidentiality purposes, the report to the full board by the board chair on the results of the performance review should only cover the highlights. Most boards will go into an executive session for this type of discussion or will leave it to the EC. This is so privacy is assured and the rest of the staff does not hear the discussion.

Once the self review and the review by the board chair have been completed, it is important for you to develop specific goals or strategies to address any negative issues identified. Be sure you document such efforts so you will be prepared to respond if the issue comes up in the next review.

Be sure copies of all documents are placed in the ED personnel file.

Salary and Benefits Tied to the ED Performance Review

Finally, the board must develop a salary review process compatible with the review process. Regardless of the strategy used, encourage your board to develop policies for determining salary increases, not only for you as the ED but also for the rest of the staff. Too often decisions about salaries are based on budget rather than on what is fair or equitable and which is comparable to ED salaries and benefits in similar-sized nonprofits.

To Recap

◆ ED performance reviews can provide valuable information on the board's perception of how the executive is doing in the achievement of strategic goals as well as fulfilling the job objectives.

◆ Board-approved policies for the ED performance review are essential to provide consistency and unbiased evaluation.

◆ The ED should complete a self-evaluation to compare with the board chair's review. Differences of opinion should be clearly noted in the executive's personnel file.

◆ The ED journal can be a great help in quantifying fulfillment of job objectives.

◆ ED salary and benefits should be tied to the performance review.

Chapter Five

ED Report to the Board

IN THIS CHAPTER

---→ Rationale for an ED report to the board

---→ Preparing for the report

---→ Collecting information for the report

---→ Presenting the report

"I think it's time we hired a new ED," the board member grumbled.

"Why do you think that?" the board chair asked.

"Every time I see the ED it seems like it is at some type of community event. Doesn't look to me like the ED is doing a bloomin' thing at the office."

Unfortunately, such conversations between board members are all too common—maybe even between your own board members. How can you keep the board informed about what you are doing without taking up the entire board meeting or writing a six-page report no one will read?

It's important for you to give frequent reports to the governing board to keep the board aware of critical administrative and community issues impacting the nonprofit that are your responsibility. But if you and your board are like most nonprofits, neither party knows what should and should not be included in the report. If your report goes into too much detail, then the board will begin to meddle into procedures, which are the responsibility of staff. If the report is too concise, the board may begin to wonder how you spend your time, and it will impact your performance evaluation.

Remember, as the ED, you are the only staff person who reports to the board, so the report must reflect not just your efforts but those of the entire staff.

Preparing for the Report

Before deciding what to include and how often to give a report, answer the following questions with the board chair's help:

❑ Should the report include strategic plan updates?

❑ Should the report include information on governance issues?

❑ What types of information on other staff should be included?

❑ Should the report include information on the receipt of major gifts or grants?

❑ Should the report outline how the ED spends time?

❑ Should the report include updates on community issues impacting the nonprofit?

❑ Should the report include information on issues identified in the annual ED performance review (see **Chapter Four**)?

If all of these issues are important to the board, it does not mean every report should include information on all of these aspects, but rather prioritize them and with the help of the board chair decide what to include in each report.

You and the board chair might decide the reports at every board meeting will include all of these issues or variations, depending on where your nonprofit is in its achievement of the mission.

For example, if a nonprofit has just hired its first ED, the board will probably want the reports to focus on the executive's efforts to achieve performance goals as outlined in their board-approved core competencies and the job description (see **Chapter Four**), which will be the basis for the performance review.

Or if the nonprofit has just completed a strategic plan, ED reports on progress toward achievement of organizational goals is important.

Sample ED Schedule

Time	Task	Core Element
8–10 a.m. (2 hours for staff development)	Staff meetings and walk around	Administration; staff development
10–11 a.m. (1 hour for board development)	Board telephone calls	Board/volunteer development
11–noon (1 hour on projects and paperwork)	Review mail and complete updates on strategic plan	Administration/paperwork/projects
Noon–1 p.m. (1 hour cultivating potential donors)	Rotary	Community involvement
1–2 p.m. (1 hour on projects and paperwork)	Work with accountant on annual budget	Administration/project/paperwork
2–3 p.m. (1 hour on projects and paperwork)	Meet with internal management director on policies and procedures manual	Administration/project/paperwork
3–4 p.m. (1 hour on projects and paperwork)	Meet with marketing director, resource development director on annual fundraising appeal	Marketing, resource dev./project/paperwork
4–5 p.m. (1 hour on projects and paperwork)	Meet with board chair regarding next board meeting's agenda	Administration/project/paperwork

Collecting Information for the Report

If you keep a daily journal (see **Chapter Four**) that indicates the amount of time spent working on each of the core elements of a successful nonprofit, you will find putting together a report for the board is very easy: Simply list major accomplishments for each of the six elements since the last report.

Just be sure to not duplicate in your report what will be reported by the board-level committees.

Sample Executive Director Report to the Board
[Date]

Administration

Financial: The CPA has started working on the books for the annual audit.

Risk Management: Bids are being collected for D&O insurance.

Facilities/Equipment: The fire marshal gave us an "A" rating after his walkthrough of the building.

Personnel: The new resource development VP will begin work next week.

Marketing

The new brand identity logo is now in use.

Publicity for the annual rubber ducky race will start next week.

Resource Development

We received a grant for $10,000 from the XYZ Foundation for the parent education program.

We received a $100,000 gift for our endowment fund.

I met with five potential endowment donors.

Programs

Staff is working on completion of the program evaluations that will be used during our annual strategic plan update in March.

Criminal background checks have been completed on all of the volunteers working with children.

Board/Volunteer Development

The volunteer development policies and procedures manual is completed, based on policies approved by the board last month.

The volunteer recognition event is scheduled for April 4.

Community Involvement

I spoke at three events: Rotary, Kiwanis, and Chamber.

Strategic Goals

All board-level committees are working with staff on the development of policies related to the six priority goals for this year.

Example

Because you will be constantly trying to balance your work load between all of the core elements (see **Appendix N**), it is critical you develop some effective time-management strategies to help you accomplish your responsibilities. And your report to the board should reflect those strategies.

Chapter six of *Nonprofit Management Simplified: Internal Operations* includes some guidelines for balancing your duties with good time-management strategies. Included in the suggestions are ways to keep track of how your time is spent.

From your journal or schedule, you will be able to put together your report to the board. An optional schedule format that combines the charting of the time spent on the core elements and strategic plan goals is included in the "Sample Time-Management Form."

Presenting the Report

Another problem associated with the ED report is the location of the report in the board meeting agenda. If it is at the beginning of the agenda and you keep the report short, it keeps what you are doing at the forefront of the board meeting.

Sample Time-Management Report

Strategic Goals	Priority Level, Estimated Time Needed	People, Projects, or Paperwork Needed	Time Needed	Core Elements Covered
A three-year marketing plan will be developed, which will increase brand identity by 30 percent.	Eight hours, plus three one-hour focus groups	Interview marketing staff person; set Marketing Committee mtg.; marketing assessment; Gary J. Stern's *Marketing Workbook for Nonprofit Organizations, Volume I*, Amherst H. Wilder Foundation (ISBN 0-940-06901-6)	◆ Two hours for committee meeting; ◆ four hours to interview, hire, and orient marketing person; ◆ two hours to complete workbook; ◆ three hours of marketing focus groups	Marketing administration volunteer development
A system of internal financial controls will be developed and implemented for testing by board members within one year.	Twelve hours	Sample financial management policies, procedures, and internal controls	◆ One hour for finance committee meeting; ◆ Two hours/day to ◆ rewrite sample policies/procedures and internal controls	Administration

However, if the report is included in the consent agenda (see **Chapter Three**), board members are apt to miss it and not read it before the meeting. Or, if the report is the last thing on the agenda, it can get lost or put off to another meeting.

Work closely with your board chair to decide the most important pieces of the written report for you to mention in your verbal report at the board meeting. Although it is easy to make the assumption board members have read the report if it is included in the consent agenda, the truth is most board members do not review the material until the meeting. So, taking five minutes at the beginning of the meeting to hit on the highlights of your report will increase the possibility board members will at least skim over the report while you are talking.

Remember, the ED's report to the board is not an appropriate time to filibuster on an issue important to you!

To Recap

- The ED's report to the board is an important tool for keeping the board informed on strategic goal achievement and the core elements.

- Use time-management strategies, journals, and other techniques for keeping track of the information you will need for preparing the report.

- Decide with the board chair on what issues are most critical to report to the board.

- Keep the verbal report to the board short and schedule it for the beginning of the meeting agenda.

Chapter Six

Volunteer Development

IN THIS CHAPTER

····→ Rational for a volunteer development plan

····→ Developing recruitment policies and procedures

····→ Developing orientation policies and procedures

····→ Developing a volunteer recognition plan

····→ Developing volunteer dismissal policies and procedures

The potential volunteer had several decades of experience as a nonprofit ED, and when after retiring, the individual decided to look for volunteer opportunities. Over a period of three years, the retiree applied to be a volunteer at several organizations without success.

One nonprofit ED was overheard telling the vice president the individual was "intimidating" because of the wealth of experience the individual had, so the ED did not want the retiree working as a volunteer at the nonprofit.

Another ED appeared eager for the retiree's help, so the retiree completed the application and even went through a criminal background check. But the nonprofit never called back following the application submission, in spite of two follow-up calls and even though the background check was spotless. The retiree never found out why.

A third nonprofit asked for the retiree's input and help on the development of two major projects. But two years later, the nonprofit's ED had done nothing to implement the projects the retiree had worked on.

The retiree gave up trying to volunteer. What a waste of talent and experience! And it was just because none of the three nonprofits had implemented volunteer development policies and procedures that would allow them to access the talents of such a high-capacity volunteer.

Rationale for a Volunteer Development Plan

Unfortunately, the retiree's experiences in trying to volunteer are not unusual. And it is often because the following strategies are often lacking in nonprofits looking for volunteers:

◆ written policies and procedures for the recruitment, training, recognition, and dismissal of volunteers

◆ a list of the types of volunteers they are looking for: board members, committee members, or program volunteers

◆ job descriptions for all volunteer positions

◆ strategies for incorporating experienced and talented volunteers (high-capacity volunteers) into its nonprofit's programs

Volunteers are, and always have been, absolutely essential to the management and programs of a nonprofit organization. Volunteers are the entrepreneurs of community building. All it takes is one volunteer with a passion for a cause and before too long there are dozens or thousands of other volunteers who catch the vision and want to be involved.

Most people have done some type of volunteer work in a nonprofit, church, or other faith-based organization (e.g., scouting, helping a neighbor, or taking a meal to a shut-in). But few people have been trained on how to be a good volunteer. Sometimes nonprofit leaders assume a spirit of altruism or passion for the mission is all the volunteers need. They also make the assumption they can expect volunteers to do whatever they need done, no questions asked.

Or nonprofits look for volunteers but they have no job descriptions for open positions, leaving the volunteer to infer by the nonprofit's lack of diligence they are just looking for warm bodies to fill an empty slot. And if the volunteer dares to ask how much time it will take, the response is often, "Oh, it won't take much time."

With more and more Baby Boomers (the post-World War II generation) retiring, these well-educated potential volunteers will not be content to stuff envelopes or serve food at an event. This type of potential volunteer is looking for opportunities to use their education and experience to support a social cause they are passionate about.

One of your important jobs as the ED is assuring the development of all volunteers, no matter what role they play in the organization. The details for implementation can be assigned to a senior staff person, but it is your responsibility to take a leadership role to insure a volunteer development program is a priority.

The development of your volunteer program can have a tremendous, long-term, positive impact on the nonprofit and on the community it serves.

It has been proven over and over again: better volunteers are also better donors. So, the development of a good volunteer program will help improve fundraising results. Establishing board-approved policies and procedures for a volunteer development program that also includes training for staff on how to work with volunteers will insure its success.

Plus, if you consciously recruit volunteers that fit into the high-capacity category, their positive impact on the organization can be tremendous. High-capacity volunteers are not only well educated but are energetic and have the potential to take on significant responsibilities beyond the scope of the nonprofit's budget for paid staff.

This chapter includes sample policies, procedures, and templates for use in developing your nonprofit's volunteer program. Not all of the policies/procedures will work for every nonprofit. These are simply examples of the types of the most common issues that must be addressed when developing a volunteer development program.

Types of Volunteers

There are basically three types of volunteers in any nonprofit, and confusion can arise when a volunteer is serving in all three roles: board, committee, and program. Make sure both volunteers and staff are trained in their roles, responsibilities, and lines of authority (see **Chapter One**).

Board of Directors

Members of the board are usually recruited for their passion or commitment to the mission of the nonprofit, because they represent a specific stakeholder, or because their community leadership or financial contribution can be a source of help to the nonprofit. The primary roles of a board member are to legally govern the nonprofit through thoughtful and workable policy setting, monitoring policy and program implementation, strategic planning, ED oversight, financial oversight, public relations, and fundraising (see **Chapter One**).

Committee Volunteers

Volunteers who act in advisory roles to board-level standing committees or task forces usually bring to the committees high degrees of expertise in specific areas. A marketing committee, for example, should be composed of volunteers with marketing and/or media background and experience. While their recommendations may eventually trigger a board policy, the committee volunteer's primary role is advice. Advisory boards are in the same category as committee volunteers.

Program Volunteers

Many volunteers perform duties that might ordinarily be done by staff. Program volunteers serve food at a soup kitchen, baby-sit for young mothers who need some time off, develop and run a fundraiser, or any of a myriad of other activities on which the nonprofit depends. The primary role of a program volunteer is to support the programs of the organization.

The board can play a significant role in volunteer development by establishing a volunteer development committee. Their development of board-approved policies related to the recruitment, training, dismissal, and recognition of all volunteers, including board members, can be extremely helpful in retaining high-capacity volunteers. Not only that, but volunteers are also the best donors to a nonprofit because they see the actual results of their contributions in the programs.

Appoint a senior staff person to handle the volunteer development program, since there are volunteers involved in every aspect and program of most nonprofits. Assigning a senior staff person reinforces the importance of the volunteer development program. If there just isn't enough money in the budget to hire a volunteer coordinator, recruit one of those high-capacity volunteers to organize the program as an unpaid staff person.

Sample Policies for Starting a Volunteer Development Program

The board will establish a volunteer development committee, based on the board-approved job description (see **Appendix C**).

The annual budget will include a line item for the volunteer development program expenses.

All volunteers will be recruited, trained, recognized and dismissed based on board-approved policies

Example

As a result of implementation of the recommended strategies, you can expect:

◆ The board will establish a volunteer development committee.

◆ A senior staff person will be assigned volunteer development responsibilities.

◆ The recruitment of all volunteers will be consistent and based on board-approved policies and staff-implemented procedures.

◆ The orientation and training of all volunteers will be a requirement and be based on board-approved policies and staff-implemented procedures.

◆ The recognition strategies for all volunteers will be based on board-approved policies and staff-implemented procedures.

◆ Dismissal policies for all volunteers will be approved by the board and implemented by the volunteers' supervisors.

◆ There will be enthusiastic, trained volunteers available to meet all of the needs of the nonprofit and staff will understand how to work with the volunteers.

◆ The turnover in volunteers will be reduced.

◆ Financial donations from volunteers will increase.

Development of Volunteer Recruitment Strategies

The following policies and procedures are samples of recruitment strategies for each of the three types of volunteers. Policies are indicated first, with tools and implementation procedures following.

Rewrite the policies to fit the needs of your nonprofit and present them to the volunteer development committee for input. The committee will then forward the final policies to the board for approval. Tools and implementation procedures can be finalized by staff at a later time as part of the development of their work plans.

Some of the examples of best practices for nonprofits related to the recruitment of all volunteers include:

◆ Volunteers are not recruited until a job description has been developed for the positions and a board-level volunteer development committee is established.

◆ Volunteers are not recruited until the board has approved policies related to the recruitment, training, recognition, and dismissal of all volunteers.

◆ Procedures developed by staff are based on the board-approved policies.

◆ A database is established and constantly updated to keep track of all the need information on volunteers and potential volunteers.

◆ Prior to the recruitment of high-capacity volunteers, the volunteer coordinator determines who will be the best person to ask these individuals to volunteer.

◆ A list is made of potential sources for volunteer recruitment, such as:

  ❖ friends and family

  ❖ service clubs

  ❖ other organizations that are volunteer driven: chambers of commerce, United Way, churches, synagogues, mosques, volunteer centers, nonprofit resource centers, RSVP, SCORE, etc.

  ❖ corporations and businesses, employees, executives

  ❖ community events, volunteer fairs, job fairs

  ❖ unions, other trade organizations

  ❖ government—local, county, state, and federal agencies

  ❖ educational and health institutions

Example

Recruitment Policies for Board Members

Chapter One includes a variety of strategies to use in the recruitment of board members. The "Sample Recruitment Policies for Board Members" below lists some sample policies you can adapt for your organization.

Sample Recruitment Policies for Board Members

Policy	Tools	Procedure
The board will appoint a nominating committee or task force to bring recommendations to the board at the meeting prior to the annual meeting (per bylaws).	**Chapter One**	Monthly or quarterly meetings will be held to review applications, term expirations of current board members, and demographic and ethnic needs for diversity.
The nominating committee/task force will work closely with the volunteer development committee to insure consistency in implementation of policies and procedures.	**Appendix C** "Job Descriptions for Committees, Committee Chairs and Vice Chairs"	Meetings will be held between the nominating committee/task force and volunteer development chairs to coordinate efforts.
A board member job description and application will be made available to all prospective board members.	**Appendix A** "Job Descriptions for Boards" **Chapter One**	Completed applications will be submitted to the nominating committee/task force.
Receipt of a completed application will not be a guarantee of acceptance, but is an expression of interest only.	**Chapter One**	Applications will be screened for demographic, ethnicity and skills; potential candidates will be interviewed; all applicants receive a letter acknowledging receipt of the application.
The nominating committee/task force will submit board member nominees for a vote at the annual members' meeting, after board approval.	**Chapter One**, "Board Matrix"	Board matrix of the entire board will be made available to show where the new board members will fill empty slots.
Board members will annually complete commitment to serve and conflict of interest statements.	**Chapter One**	Staff will keep files on all board members and include signed copies of commitment to serve and conflict of interest statements.

Recruitment Policies for Committee Volunteers

Board standing committees should be limited to no more than six. Too many committees and the work can become fragmented. A sample "Core Elements Committee Structure" for a small nonprofit is shown in **Chapter One**. Larger nonprofits could divide the three committees into six, based on the "Core Elements Chart," **Chapter Two**.

Remember, board-level committees can include community members who have the potential to be board members. Board members involved in board member recruitment can watch committee members in action to see if they might be good candidates for board membership.

Sample Recruitment Policies for Committee Volunteers

Policy	Tools	Procedure
The chair and vice chair of all board-appointed committees will be board members and will be appointed at the first board meeting of the fiscal year, per the bylaws.	**Appendix C**, "Job Descriptions for Committees, Committee Chairs and Vice Chairs"	All committee chairs and vice chairs will receive copies of their job descriptions.
All board members will sit on at least one board standing committee.	"Core Elements Committee Structure," **Chapter One**	At the first board meeting of the fiscal year, board members will select the committee on which they will serve.
Committee work will be based on board-approved committee job descriptions.	**Appendix C** "Job Descriptions for Committees, Committee Chairs and Vice Chairs"	All committee members will be given copies of the committee job descriptions.
Additional members of the committees can be community volunteers with expertise in specific areas to assist the committees in their work.	**Appendix C** "Job Descriptions for Board-Level Committees and Committee Chairs and Vice Chairs"	Potential committee members who are community volunteers will be given a copy of the committee job description.
Community volunteers will complete a volunteer application prior to their acceptance as a member of a board standing committee.	"Sample Volunteer Application"	Potential committee members who are community volunteers will be given a volunteer application to complete.
Community volunteers will sign a commitment to serve and conflict of interest statement before serving on a board standing committee.	"Sample Volunteer Commitment to Serve Form"	All committee members who are community volunteers will sign a commitment to serve and a conflict of interest statement.

Recruitment Policies for Program Volunteers

Nonprofits depend on program volunteers to carry out the myriad activities geared toward fulfillment of the mission. Solid recruitment strategies and policies for program volunteers are critical to not only the success of the programs but also for the fulfillment of the volunteers' personal objectives.

Volunteer Application

When all volunteers (board, committee, and program) complete applications, not only does the nonprofit have a better idea where to place the volunteer, but volunteers better understand their roles and responsibilities, especially when the application is coupled with a job description of potential duties.

The sample policies provide consistency in the recruitment and also prevent potential problems such as abuse or other criminal behavior. Adapt the sample policies to the various types of volunteers involved in programs. No sample job descriptions are included for program volunteers since their duties vary so greatly and depend on the type of nonprofit and programs.

Sample Volunteer Application for Committee and Program Volunteers

In order to be considered as volunteer, the volunteer application* needs to be completed and submitted to the volunteer development coordinator. The purpose of the application is to match the volunteer with appropriate volunteer opportunities.

	☑	
Indicate with a check mark the current status of the volunteer.		Volunteer is already volunteering for the nonprofit as: (position/duties)
		Potential volunteer has received a copy of a job description for: (position)
		Volunteer has worked with other nonprofits: (list with position/duties)
Date		
Person interviewing volunteer		
Potential volunteer information		
Name		
Preferred mailing address		
E-mail/website		
Daytime phone number		
Age (optional)		
Occupation		
Preferred title		
Place of employment		
Ethnicity (optional)		
Education/training		
Strengths or skills the volunteer would bring to the nonprofit		

"If I am selected as a volunteer, I agree to adhere to all the volunteer policies and procedures, including policies related to dismissal, confidentiality, and criminal background checks."

Signature:_____ Date:_____

*Each volunteer will complete and submit a volunteer application to the volunteer development coordinator. The information will be entered into a database to provide the necessary orientation and recognition information. All supervisors (staff and volunteer) will keep good records on who volunteers to do what. Such records will be kept confidential. Only the supervisor, governing board, and person entering the data will have access to it.

Job descriptions are not needed for mundane activities like sweeping the floor, but develop job descriptions for all positions that need specific skills or experience, such as answering the phone, working with clients, or doing database entry.

Sample Recruitment Policies for Program Volunteers

Policy	Tool	Procedure
All program volunteers will complete a volunteer application and be given a job description when appropriate.	"Sample Volunteer Application"	Recruit volunteers; give potential volunteers job descriptions and applications.
Criminal background checks will be conducted on any program volunteer who will have contact with vulnerable clients (children, youth, disabled, or elderly).	Criminal background form provided by the city, county, or state	Submit criminal background check form; advise volunteer when results are received.
Program volunteers working with clients will be paired with an experienced volunteer or staff person for at least six months to monitor their work and identify potential problems.		
Each program volunteer will be supervised and evaluated at least annually by a staff person.	Evaluation form developed by supervisor	Evaluate volunteers.

Another key document that can be used use during the recruitment phase of your volunteer development strategies is the "Commitment to Serve Form." You can use the same form for confidentiality and conflict of interest statements, as shown, or incorporate the statements into the application.

Commitment Forms

When all volunteers annually sign commitment to serve forms, the nonprofit and the volunteers have the opportunity to evaluate the position the volunteer is serving in and whether or not there is a need for change. See the opposite page for a sample of the Commitment to Serve Form.

Development of Orientation Policies and Procedures

The purpose of volunteer orientations is to inform new board members, officers, and committee and program volunteers about the nonprofit's history, structure, and mission as well as to:

◆ orient volunteers to their responsibilities and their relationships to other volunteers

◆ provide continuity in the information in order to more effectively fulfill the mission and objectives of your nonprofit

Orientations of all volunteers should include the following elements:

◆ history and mission of the nonprofit

◆ organizational structure

◆ bylaws, values, policies, and procedures (as they relate to the ability of the volunteer to fulfill their responsibilities)

◆ organizational objectives

◆ strategic plan goals

◆ issues impacting the nonprofit and its ability to provide services to clients

◆ job descriptions and responsibilities of the volunteer, including evaluations and dismissal policies

- ◆ roles, responsibilities, and lines of authority for all volunteers

- ◆ leadership development (where appropriate or needed)

- ◆ external relationships with other nonprofits or organizations

- ◆ volunteer recognition (during the orientation, ask the volunteers what types of recognition they prefer, such as plaques, verbal recognition, no recognition, etc.)

Sample Commitment to Serve Form	
"I do hereby declare and affirm my willingness to assume the responsibilities, as stated in the job description, and to abide by the following guidelines:"	
Guideline	**Explanation**
Confidentiality	To adhere to the strictest confidentiality related to any and all client or nonprofit information, unless there is illegal activity, and to submit to a criminal background check if needed.
Dismissal	To adhere to the policies related to volunteer dismissal.
Conflict of Interest	No volunteer shall knowingly take any action or make any statement intended to influence the conduct of the nonprofit in such a way as to confer any financial or personal benefit on such member or the member's family or on any corporation in which the member is an employee or has a significant interest as stockholder, director, or officer, with which the member may serve as a director or trustee or in a professional capacity. In the event there comes before the committee a matter for consideration or decision that raises a potential conflict of interest for any member of the committee, the member shall disclose the conflict of interest as soon as the member becomes aware of it, and the disclosure shall be recorded in the minutes of the meeting as part of the voting record. Any member of the committee who is aware of a potential conflict of interest with respect to any matter coming before the committee shall not vote in connection with the matter nor will the member's presence at the meeting (electronic or in person) be counted in determining whether a quorum exists. These guidelines are not intended to prevent or discourage any member of the committee from disclosing relevant information with respect to any matter to which the member has knowledge or from answering questions or stating the member's position with respect to any such matter.
Acknowledgement	*"I, _____, a volunteer for (nonprofit), have read the guidelines with respect to potential conflicts of interest and the commitment to serve and agree to comply therewith. Further, I understand my continuing obligation of disclosure of potential conflict of interest should circumstances or events so warrant. I understand any expenses associated with attendance at events or meetings are my sole responsibility, unless prior approval has been given by the governing board or supervisor.*

_____

(*signature*)   (*date*)

The "Types of Orientations" chart gives examples of who is responsible for orientations and when the orientations will be done. A more-detailed training agenda for board members is available in **Chapter One**.

Types of Orientations

	Board Members	Committee Volunteers	Program Volunteers
Type of orientation	Two-hour group training, mini-trainings at board meetings, and/or one-on-one orientations (see **Chapter One**)	Meeting effectiveness, committee responsibilities (see **Appendix C**), meeting effectiveness (see **Chapter One**) and overview of nonprofit	Task instructions and overview of nonprofit
Trainer	Outside facilitator, past board chair, or ED	Committee chair or ED	Supervisor of the volunteer
Timeline	When approved as a board member and annually thereafter or mini-trainings at each board meeting	When brought on to the committee and annually thereafter	When recruited and at least annually thereafter

Orientation Agendas

Although the types of orientations and the information included will vary from nonprofit to nonprofit, the "Sample Orientation Agendas" includes the primary components of a typical agenda.

Board Orientation

Typical agenda for board members, committee members, and program volunteers will generally include the components listed below. For more information and a more-detailed agenda, see **Chapter One.**

◆ 5 min.: Welcome and introductions

◆ 15 min.: History, purpose, mission, and programs of the nonprofit

◆ 15 min: Purpose and functions of the governing board of directors

  ❖ types of boards

  ❖ definition of policy

◆ 1 hr.: Roles, responsibilities, and lines of authority for a board member (see **Chapter One**)

  ❖ legal

  ❖ policies

  ❖ financial

  ❖ program

  ❖ planning

  ❖ fundraising

- ❖ oversight of the ED

- ❖ public relations

◆ 20 min.: Effective boards

- ❖ structure

- ❖ recruitment, training, dismissal, and recognition

- ❖ effective meetings

- ❖ strategic planning and evaluation

◆ 5 min.: Wrap-up

Committee and Program Volunteer Orientation Agenda (70 minutes):

◆ 5 min.: Welcome and introductions

◆ 10 min.: History, purpose, and programs of the nonprofit

◆ 10 min.: Purpose and functions of the board and officers

◆ 15 min.: Roles, responsibilities, and lines of authority (**Chapter One**)

◆ 25 min.: Effective volunteers

- ❖ job descriptions

- ❖ effective meetings

- ❖ evaluation and dismissal policies

◆ 5 min.: Wrap-up

A good volunteer development program will not only include policies and procedures for recruitment and orientation but also for recognition and dismissal strategies.

Development of a Volunteer Recognition Plan

Most state laws define volunteers as individuals receiving $500 or fewer per year in any type of remuneration (including recognition awards), except for reimbursement of expenses. So make sure your recognition efforts do not exceed your state's financial requirements of volunteer remuneration.

One of the difficulties associated with providing satisfactory recognition for volunteers is the reasons why people volunteer are very different. As a result, the types of recognition must vary. There are volunteers who will be offended if the nonprofit spends any money on recognition items. They would rather have the money spent for services than for plaques. Other volunteers like to be able to put a plaque on their wall or to see an article in the newsletter.

It is important, therefore, to know what types of recognition each volunteer will appreciate. Do not forget expenditures for tangible recognition items (e.g., gifts, plaques) must be approved by the ED and/or the board if they are not a part of the board-approved budget.

Volunteer Recognition Policies
A volunteer development coordinator will bring recommended recognition policies to the volunteer development committee for their review, and the committee will then take the policies to the board for final approval.
Information in the volunteer database will be confidential and accessible only by the ED and the volunteer development coordinator.
All volunteers (board, committee, and program) will be recognized for their efforts at the annual meeting.
Funding for any tangible recognition items will be included in the annual budget.

One of the most critical components of a good volunteer recognition plan is a good database of information on all volunteers. Below is a suggested list of items to include in any volunteer database:

◆ name

◆ address

◆ contact information (including emergency contact)

◆ year when the person began volunteering

◆ listing of all of the individual's volunteer jobs

◆ when the volunteer attended orientations or trainings

◆ supervisors

◆ job descriptions

◆ recognitions given and when

◆ types of recognition preferred

◆ copies of any evaluations completed by the volunteer and the supervisor

Be creative. Recognition does not have to be expensive. Types of recognition other than plaques might include:

◆ Call the volunteer at home to express your appreciation.

◆ Send a handwritten note of thanks; have the chair of the nonprofit board or ED sign the note.

◆ Recognize volunteers at the annual membership meeting.

◆ Nominate the volunteer for a local, state, or national award (like the J.C. Penney Golden Rule Award).

◆ Make sure any milestones or achievements are listed on the website or other communications.

◆ Provide donuts or other snacks for the volunteers at meetings.

◆ When appropriate, show interest in the volunteer's work or home life.

◆ Give tokens of appreciation: balloons, flowers, candy, book, poster, plaques, awards, etc.

◆ Name an annual award after a long-time, key volunteer.

◆ Establish endowments in the names of key volunteers.

◆ Have children/clients in the program do handwritten thank-you notes or pictures.

◆ Above all, just say "thanks" every chance you get!

Sample Recognition Strategies

	Board Members	Committee Volunteers	Program Volunteers
Purpose of the Recognition	To show appreciation for commitment and support	To show appreciation for commitment and support	To show appreciation for commitment and support
Responsibility	Nominating committee/ task force or volunteer development coordinator	Volunteer development coordinator and committee chair	Volunteer development coordinator and supervisor
Elements	At election as board member and completion of term; acceptance or completion of office; any community recognition	At beginning and end of service on the committee; special accomplishments	At beginning of service and at one-year intervals thereafter; at completion of service
Type	Gifts, plaques, letters	Gifts, plaques, letters	Gifts, plaques, letters

Development of Dismissal Policies and Procedures

Because volunteers are so important to most nonprofits, providing unpaid service that keeps the nonprofit's expenses low, many nonprofit employees believe firing or dismissing a volunteer is not possible.

If, however, the volunteer is viewed as unpaid staff and treated in the same way as staff, with trainings and evaluations, then it is easier to understand firing a volunteer is much like firing a staff person. The three steps to take in dismissing a volunteer must be just as meticulous as the steps for firing paid staff:

◆ To avoid frequent dismissals of volunteers, make sure when volunteers are recruited they understand they will be evaluated and can be dismissed if the fit is not right with the nonprofit.

◆ Develop policies and procedures related to the evaluation process for volunteers so not only does the supervisor evaluate the volunteer but the volunteer should be able to also evaluate the supervisor.

◆ Be careful in the firing procedures so it does not create more problems than the volunteer is creating.

Remember these are not legal opinions but suggestions, and all policies related to dismissal should be reviewed by an attorney familiar with nonprofits and nonprofit law.

"Sample Dismissal Policies and Procedures" is an example of dismissal policies and procedures that will be helpful as you develop your own. There are several policies and procedures that should be in place to ease the trauma of firing volunteers.

Sample Dismissal Policies and Procedures

By approving dismissal policies and procedures for all volunteers (board, committee, and program), not only is the nonprofit clarifying responsibilities and improving community but such policies can also go a long way toward diminishing potential conflict.

Sample Volunteer Dismissal Policies

We believe if there has been proper recruitment and training of volunteers, there should be no need to dismiss a volunteer for any reason. However, situations may arise where volunteers are just not a good fit to a particular position or there is illegal activity, such as harassment or abuse.

All volunteers serving in positions with job descriptions will be asked to sign a "Commitment to Serve" that includes an overview of their responsibilities, confidentiality, and conflict of interest statements and an agreement the volunteer will adhere to the dismissal policies and procedures.

Every effort will be made to keep any dismissals as confidential as possible, unless there is illegal activity.

The nonprofit reserves the right to dismiss volunteers and will use the following procedures:

Behavior	Policy/Procedure
Illegal Activity or Improper Conduct by a Volunteer	◆ If a volunteer is accused of illegal activity, the proper legal authorities will be contacted immediately and the volunteer will be placed on indefinite suspension from the volunteer position(s) until such time as the charges are proven false. ◆ If the volunteer is convicted of the charges, the volunteer will be permanently suspended from holding a volunteer position within the nonprofit. The nonprofit's crisis communication plan will be implemented to respond to inquiries by the media. ◆ If a volunteer is accused of improper conduct, the volunteer will meet one-on-one with the staff or volunteer supervisor and with a member of the senior management team. The meeting will be confidential and those in attendance will make every attempt to resolve the situation in a respectful manner. ◆ If there is belligerence or unwillingness on the part of the volunteer to amicably resolve the situation, the volunteer will be removed from the volunteer position. The volunteer will not be given a different volunteer position unless the volunteer is paired with another volunteer for mentoring and training.
Improper Fit of the Volunteer with a Specific Position	◆ All volunteers will be trained in their volunteer activities and be mentored for one year by a designated supervisor or experienced volunteer. ◆ If, at any time or for any reason during the one year, the volunteer or the volunteer's mentor determines the volunteer position is not a good fit, the volunteer may be dismissed. ◆ Every attempt will be made to place the volunteer in another more appropriate position

Because volunteers have such critical roles in every nonprofit, establishing board-approved policies and staff-implemented procedures will not only enhance the volunteer development program but it will also expand the capacity of the nonprofit to meet needs within their community.

To Recap

Volunteer development is critical to the success of any nonprofit; the establishment of policies and procedures related to the following items will increase the success of the volunteer development program:

- ◆ a board-level volunteer development committee
- ◆ recruitment policies and procedures for board, committee, and program volunteers
- ◆ orientation policies and procedures for board, committee, and program volunteers
- ◆ recognition policies and procedures for board, committee, and program volunteers
- ◆ dismissal policies and procedures for board, committee, and program volunteers

Appendix A: Boards of Directors Sample Job Descriptions

Advisory Board Member

Reports to

The advisory board member reports to a governing board of directors.

Selected by

Advisory board members are usually appointed by specific agencies, entities, or individuals to represent their opinions and viewpoints to the governing board of directors.

Term

The term may be ongoing, with no specific term, or may be specific to the needs of the governing or advisory boards.

Attendance

Attendance usually depends upon the tasks assigned to the advisory board. Specific attendance policies should be implemented.

Responsibilities

◆ *Demographic representation*—responsible for representing the interests of the nonprofit, entity, or individual who appointed the advisory board member

◆ *Advisory*—does not set policy but recommends actions or policies to the governing board and/or staff

◆ *Education*—takes the initiative to become knowledgeable about the nonprofit, programs, and policies of the organization

◆ *Communication*—maintains open communication with staff and other advisory board members

♦ *Support*—provides positive support of the organization to the general public

♦ *Research*—conducts necessary research or study to support input to the board

Expenses

Any expenses associated with the position are generally covered by the appointing entity.

Time Commitment

The time commitment varies but generally is one to two hours a month.

Administrative Board Member

Selected by

Because administrative boards are generally start-up boards or are involved with organizations with no paid staff, members are usually self-selected initially but can also be recruited by other start-up or charter board members.

Term

While a limitation of terms is generally desirable, start-up administrative boards usually do not have terms until the organization hires its first staff. Recommended terms would be three 2-year terms or two 3-year terms.

Attendance Requirements

Given the lack of staff, administrative boards often meet on a daily or weekly basis. Attendance at such meetings should be mandatory, with resignations accepted after missing two to three meetings in a row.

Responsibilities

Because there is no staff in the organization, administrative boards function as unpaid staff, the governing board, and an advisory board. Responsibilities may include (but are not limited to) the following:

♦ *Policy*—to consider, approve, and support management policies that promote and enhance the mission of the organization

♦ *Public relations*—to represent the nonprofit to the general public, including speaking presentations to potential donors or foundations

♦ *Fundraising*—to plan, execute, and evaluate all fundraising efforts

♦ *Management*—to assure development, execution, and evaluation of solid infrastructure systems, such as financial management; facilities; program development; marketing; volunteer recruitment; recognition and training; community involvement; strategic, long-range planning; and evaluation systems

♦ *Transition*—to assist in moving the organization to the point of hiring staff and, once staff is hired, to assist in moving the board to a governing board and to moving away from administrative oversight

♦ Commitment to contribute time, money, and resources

◆ to prepare for meetings or administrative tasks by reading background material and soliciting assistance from similar agencies or programs

◆ to avoid conflicts of interest and, if such a conflict does arise, to declare the conflict to the board and refrain from voting on relevant issues.

Expenses

Since there is no paid staff, administrative expenses of board members are often paid (e.g., postage, copying, purchase of supplies, etc.), although travel, meals, and time are usually not paid to the volunteer board.

Time Commitment

Time commitment varies, depending on the number of other board members involved. If acting as a start-up administrative board, it could involve one to two hours per week.

Governing Board Member

Selected by

Governing board members are nominated and selected by current members of the governing board.

Term

The term is generally three 2-year terms but not to exceed six years total without the board member taking at least one year off of the board.

Attendance

Member is required to attend a minimum of 50 percent of the scheduled meetings per year. Unexcused absence from two consecutive meetings constitutes a resignation (per the bylaws).

Responsibilities

As stated in the corporate bylaws;

"The affairs of the Corporation shall be managed by its Board of Directors. . . ."

◆ *Policy*—to consider, approve, and support management policies that promote and enhance the mission of the organization

◆ *Public relations*—to report to and represent the organization in a positive manner to the general public

◆ *Fundraising*—to support the organization with personal contributions and to actively participate in the raising of funds to support the organization

◆ *Advisory*—to act as an advisor to the staff by serving on at least one board committee

◆ *Legal*—to exercise fiduciary and legal responsibility for the affairs of the corporation

◆ *Planning*—to develop and monitor short- and long-term strategic plans that enhance and support the vision and mission of the organization

◆ *ED Oversight*—to recruit, train, supervise, and terminate the ED

◆ *Fiduciary*—to assure the nonprofit meets the basic standards of accounting for nonprofits and that the financial policies and procedures are followed by staff; to assure the financial stability of the nonprofit

Commitment

◆ To contribute to discussions at meetings, having read background materials, and to contribute individual skills and resources as appropriate

◆ To observe parliamentary procedures (can specify use of the "Simplified Parliamentary Procedures" as shown in **Chapter Three**)

◆ To avoid intruding into administrative issues that is the responsibility of the staff, except to assure their adherence to policy

◆ To avoid conflicts of interest and, if such conflict does arise, to declare the conflict to the board and refrain from voting on relevant items

◆ To attend governing board meetings, committee meetings, annual meetings, and other events that enhance board skills and knowledge

Expenses

Any expenses associated with attendance at events or meetings are the sole responsibility of the board member.

Time Commitment

The member is required to attend a minimum of 50 percent of scheduled meetings, plus the annual meeting and other special events or fundraisers. At a minimum, board membership will require two to four hours per month.

Appendix B—Board and Staff Roles and Responsibilities Quiz

Instructions

Indicate who is primarily responsible for the action:

- ◆ board
- ◆ staff (includes ED)
- ◆ both board and staff

Responsibility	*Who is Responsible?
Planning	
Determine basic purpose/goals of nonprofit	
Determine which nonprofit needs should be met and to what extent	
Determine categories of service to be provided	
Determine long-range plans for nonprofit	
Develop programs to meet needs	
Set specific program objectives	
Determine funding level needed	
Develop program and management evaluation systems, including outcomes measurements	

Responsibility	*Who is Responsible?
Policy	
Provide background information	
Give input to policy	
Make policy	
Resource Development	
Develop resource development plan	
Develop funding sources	
Solicit funds and other resources	
Evaluate fundraising success	
Financial Management	
Prepare nonprofit budget	
Monitor how funds are spent each day	
Monitor total funding picture	
Hire CPA for audit	
Personnel and Volunteer Policies	
Determine personnel and volunteer policies	
Recruit, screen, hire, supervise, terminate, evaluate, provide training opportunities for ED	
Recruit, screen, hire, supervise, terminate, evaluate, provide training opportunities for paid staff	
Recruit, screen, hire, supervise, terminate, evaluate, provide training opportunities for board members	
Recruit, screen, hire, supervise, terminate, evaluate, provide training opportunities for committee members	
Recruit, screen, hire, supervise, terminate, evaluate, provide training opportunities for program volunteers	

Responsibility	*Who is Responsible?
Marketing	
Identify the brand of the nonprofit	
Develop a formal marketing/public relations plan	
Implement marketing/public relations plan	
Serve on the boards of other nonprofits	
Maintain contact with state, national entities	

Board/Staff Roles & Responsibilities Quiz—Answers

Responsibility	*Who is Responsible?
Planning	
Determine basic purpose/goals of nonprofit	Board
Determine which nonprofit needs should be met and extent	Board
Determine categories of service to be provided	Board
Determine long-range plans for nonprofit	Board
Develop programs to meet needs	Staff
Set specific program objectives	Staff
Determine funding level needed	Staff
Develop program and management evaluation systems, including outcomes measurements	Staff
Policy	
Provide background information	Staff
Give input to policy	Both
Make policy	Board
Resource Development	
Develop resource development plan	Both
Develop funding sources	Both
Solicit funds and other resources	Both
Evaluate fundraising success	Both
Financial Management	
Prepare nonprofit budget	Staff
Monitor how funds are spent each day	Staff

Responsibility	*Who is Responsible?
Monitor total funding picture	Board
Hire CPA for audit	Board
Personnel and Volunteer Policies	
Determine personnel and volunteer policies	Board
Recruit, screen, hire, supervise, terminate, evaluate, provide training opportunities for ED	Board
Recruit, screen, hire, supervise, terminate, evaluate, provide training opportunities for paid staff	Staff
Recruit, screen, hire, supervise, terminate, evaluate, provide training opportunities for board members	Board (with ED input)
Recruit, screen, hire, supervise, terminate, evaluate, provide training opportunities for committee members	Both
Recruit, screen, hire, supervise, terminate, evaluate, provide training opportunities for program volunteers	Staff
Marketing	
Identify the brand of the nonprofit	Board
Develop a formal marketing/public relations plan	Staff
Implement marketing/public relations plan	Staff
Serve on the boards of other nonprofits	Both*
Maintain contact with state, national entities	Both*
*As long as there is no conflict of interest	

Appendix C—Sample Job Descriptions for Board-Level Committees and Committee Chairs and Vice Chairs

Executive Committee

Responsible to

Board of Directors

Purpose of Committee

The purpose of the committee is to act in the board's place between board meetings and to evaluate potential policies and board recommendations to assure their adherence to the bylaws, mission, goals, and strategic plan of the organization (see bylaws).

Key Responsibilities

◆ *Strategic planning*—to develop, update, and monitor the implementation of a strategic, long-range plan for the organization, assuring input from all divisions/committees and staff

◆ *Policy updates*—to periodically review and update as needed the bylaws, policies, and any other legal documents

◆ *Review committees' recommendations*—to review all recommended policies and procedures from the committees before they are presented to the board to assure their adherence to the organization's mission, goals, and strategic plan

◆ *Board communication*—to keep the board of directors informed of any decisions made or contracts signed between board meetings and to bring policy decisions to the board for approval or ratification;

◆ ED reviews—to annually review the performance of the ED, to report the results of the performance review to the board, and to make any recommendations regarding salary or benefits

◆ Potential board members—with the assistance of the volunteer development committee, to recommend to the board, board members for the annual nomination process

Committee Structure

The chair of the board shall serve as the chair of the executive committee (see bylaws). The committee shall be composed of the officers and the chair and vice chair of each of the standing committees/divisions. Subcommittees or short-term task force groups may be formed to complete the objectives of the committee.

Time Commitment

The time commitment is at least one meeting per month or as needed to fulfill the committee's goals.

Nominating Task Force or Committee

Responsible to

The board-level committee responsible for volunteer development will act as the nominating task force or will appoint such a task force. The nominating task force will be approved by and report to the board of directors.

Membership

The nominating task force will have a majority of its members from the board of directors. At the discretion of the board-level committee, representatives from the client base may be added to the task force. Total membership on the task force shall be no more than ten and no less than five. The chair of the task force will be the immediate past chair of the board of directors. The ED shall be a nonvoting, ex-officio member of the task force.

Strategies/Timeline:

This is based on the nonprofit's fiscal year.

◆ *September:* Nominating task force is appointed by the volunteer development committee or executive committee and approved by the board of directors.

◆ *October/November:* Nominating task force develops a slate of officers and members of the board of directors, contacting each potential candidate for their acceptance of the nomination.

◆ *December:* Nominating task force presents a slate of officers to the board of directors for approval.

◆ *February:* Slate of officers and board members presents to the membership for approval at the annual meeting, at which time they begin their terms of office.

Vacancies on the Board

Between annual meetings, any vacancies on the board of directors will be filled only if total board membership drops below twenty (maximum board membership is twenty-five, per the bylaws).

Volunteer Development Committee

Responsible to

Board of Directors

Purpose of Committee

The purpose of the committee is to assure the fulfillment of the board-approved policies and to advise staff on issues related to the recruitment, recognition, dismissal, and training of all volunteers for the fulfillment of the organization's mission and objectives, including committee, program, and board volunteers.

Key Responsibilities

◆ *Planning*—to develop short- and long-range goals and action steps related to the recruitment, training, dismissal, and recognition of all nonprofit volunteers, including committee, program, and board volunteers

◆ *Resource and needs assessments*—to assess organizational volunteer resources available and needed to fulfill the mission and goals

◆ *Recruitment*—to develop and implement the procedures needed for the recruitment of volunteers who will represent the diversity of the community and who will be effective in the fulfillment of the organization's mission and goals; to serve as the nominating task force if the executive committee so chooses

◆ *Training*—to develop and implement the orientation and training methods needed to prepare all volunteers for their duties and which will develop leadership within the organization and for the community

◆ *Recognition*—to develop and implement the variety of methods for recognition of staff, volunteers, donors, and funded agencies or programs and to develop and implement policies and procedures related to fair and equitable treatment of all volunteers

◆ *Board communication*—to keep the board of directors informed on the implemented strategies, results of volunteer development efforts, and any potential policies needed that will allow for efficient and effective volunteer development

Committee Structure

The chair of the committee shall be a member of the board of directors and shall select, or cause to be selected, a vice chair. The chair will also serve as a member of the executive committee and shall keep the board informed on the committee's progress on board-approved goals. A majority of the committee shall be board members. Subcommittees or short-term task force groups may be formed to complete the committee's objectives.

Time Commitment

The time commitment is at least one meeting per month or as needed to fulfill the committee's goals.

(Note: In smaller communities, the consolidation of the Administration and Volunteer Development Committees is feasible.)

Administration Committee or Internal Management Committee

Responsible to

Board of Directors

Purpose of Committee

The purpose of the committee is to develop policies and monitoring of year-round internal controls for management excellence and to provide advice to staff on the implementation of policies.

Key Responsibilities

◆ *Planning*—to develop short- and long-range goals and advise the staff on action steps for goal completion

◆ *Resource and needs assessments*—to assess community, volunteer, staff, and internal resources available and needed to support internal management in the most efficient and effective manner possible

◆ *Finance*—to develop and monitor policies and procedures for internal financial management that conform to standards of accounting for nonprofits and that meet all governmental regulations and requirements

◆ *Legal*—to develop and monitor policies and procedures for risk management that conform to nonprofit standards and prevent harm to volunteers, staff, and the organization

◆ *Facilities*—to provide for the procurement, upkeep, and policies related to the facilities and to assure quality facilities adequate for the completion of the nonprofit's mission

◆ *Technology/equipment*—to evaluate and procure equipment suitable for the efficient and effective fulfillment of the mission and objectives of the organization

◆ *Human resources*—to develop and monitor policies and procedures related to employment of staff that conform to all governmental regulations and provide for equitable treatment of employees

◆ *Risk management*—to annually review the insurance needs of the nonprofit and its programs, to develop safety and disaster plans and policies, and to make recommendations to the board for any additions or needed changes

◆ *Board communications*—to keep the board of directors informed on the implemented strategies, results of administrative efforts, and any potential policies needed that will allow for efficient and effective internal management that meets total quality management standards

Committee Structure

The chair of the committee shall be a member of the board of directors and shall select, or cause to be selected, a vice chair. The chair and vice chair shall also serve as members of the executive committee and shall keep the board informed on the committee's oversight of board-approved, committee goals. A majority of the committee shall be board members. Subcommittees or short-term task force groups may be formed to complete the committee's objectives. The treasurer and assistant treasurer shall be members of the committee.

Time Commitment

The time commitment is at least one meeting per month or as needed to fulfill the committee's goals.

(Note: In smaller communities, consolidation of Administration and Board/Volunteer Development Committees is feasible.)

Marketing Committee

Responsible to

Board of Directors

Purpose of Committee

The purpose of the committee is to develop and monitor policies related to year-round strategies to convey the image and information that enhance and promote the vision, mission, and goals of the nonprofit and to advise the staff on relevant strategies.

Key Responsibilities

- *Planning*—to develop short- and long-term year-round marketing goals and to advise staff on action steps for their fulfillment

- *Resource assessment*—to assess community, volunteer, staff, and financial resources needed to fulfill marketing plans

- *Publicity*—to approve or develop (if no paid staff in the position) publicity materials for all communication media, which will:

  - educate donors, potential donors, and recipients on the vision, mission, goals, and effectiveness of the organization and the programs provided;

  - convince past and potential donors to make contributions of time and money;

  - thank donors and the community for their support;

  - promote special events or volunteer opportunities.

- *Image enhancement*—to develop and monitor:

  - events or other strategies that will enhance the positive image of the nonprofit

  - a "look" that consistently conveys the approved image of the nonprofit on all correspondence, awards, newsletter, etc.

- *Brand identity*—the development of a "brand" that conveys to donors, potential donors, and all other stakeholders the unique of the mission, including needed research to verify the brand/image is having an impact through the marketing strategies

- *Board communication*—to keep the board informed on the implemented strategies, results of marketing efforts, and any potential policies needed, such as policies related to crisis communication

Committee Structure

The chair of the committee shall be a member of the board of directors and shall select, or cause to be selected, a vice chair. The chair and vice chair shall also serve as members of the executive committee, and shall keep the board informed on the committee's oversight of board-approved, committee goals. A majority of the committee shall be board members. Subcommittees or short-term task force groups may be formed to complete the committee's objectives.

Time Commitment

The time commitment is at least one meeting per month or as needed to fulfill the committee's goals.

(Note: In smaller communities, consolidation of Marketing and Resource Development Committees is feasible.)

Resource Development Committee

Responsible to

Board of Directors

Purpose of the Committee

The purpose of the committee is to develop policies and to monitor the implementation of year-round strategies related to procurement of financial and nonfinancial resources necessary to fulfill the vision, mission, and goals of the organization and to advise staff on implementation of policies and procedures.

Key Responsibilities

◆ *Planning*—to develop short- and long-term year-round resource development goals and to advise staff on action steps for their fulfillment

◆ *Resource assessment*—to assess community, volunteer, staff, and financial resources needed to fulfill resource development goals

◆ *Research*—to research, develop, evaluate, and monitor innovative strategies to procure resources from untapped markets

◆ *Fundraising*—to conduct the annual fundraising campaign, including leadership giving strategies for the board and donors

◆ *Gifts-in-Kind*—to develop and monitor strategies to procure and disburse noncash items for use by the nonprofit

◆ *Grants*—to develop and monitor strategies to procure grants for the nonprofit

◆ *Planned giving*—to develop and monitor strategies to procure gifts of cash and property through a variety of planned giving tools

◆ *Board communication*—to keep the board informed on the implemented strategies, results of resource development efforts, and any potential policies needed

Committee Structure

The chair of the committee shall be a member of the board of directors and shall select, or cause to be selected, a vice chair. The chair and vice chair shall also serve as members of the executive committee, and shall keep the board informed on the committee's oversight of board-approved, committee goals. A majority of the committee shall be board members. Subcommittees or short-term task force groups may be formed to complete the committee's objectives.

Time Commitment

The time commitment is at least one meeting per month or as needed to fulfill the committee's goals.

(Note: In smaller communities, consolidation of Marketing and Resource Development Committees is feasible.)

Program Committee

Responsible to

Board of Directors

Purpose of Committee

The purpose of the committee is to develop policies and provide advice to staff on strategies related to the implementation of board-approved programs and to evaluate and recommend any changes in overall programs, program goals, and measurable program outcomes.

Key Responsibilities

◆ *Planning*—to develop short- and long-term year-round program goals and to advise staff on action steps for their fulfillment, including outcomes measurements

◆ *Resource assessment*—to assess community, volunteer, staff, and financial resources needed to fulfill program goals

◆ *Research*—to develop, evaluate, and monitor innovative strategies for programs

◆ *Board communication*—to keep the board informed on the implemented strategies, results of program efforts ,and any potential policies needed

Committee Structure

The chair of the committee shall be a member of the board of directors and shall select, or cause to be selected, a vice chair. The chair and vice chair shall also serve as members of the executive committee, and shall keep the board informed on the committee's oversight of board-approved, committee goals. A majority of the committee shall be board members. Subcommittees or short-term task force groups may be formed to complete the committee's objectives.

Time Commitment

The time commitment is at least one meeting per month or as needed to fulfill the committee's goals.

(Note: In smaller communities, consolidation of Program and Community Involvement Committees is feasible.)

Community Involvement or Community-building Committee

Responsible to

Board of Directors

Purpose of Committee

The purpose of the committee is to develop policies and provide advice to staff on the implementation of policies and all activities related to the nonprofit's involvement in building a safe and healthy community and the building of workable collaborations.

Key Responsibilities

◆ *Planning*—to develop short- and long-term year-round goals for the nonprofit's involvement in the community; to advise staff on action steps for their fulfillment, including outcome measurements

◆ *Needs and resource assessments*—to assess community, program, volunteer, staff, and financial resources needed to fulfill community-building goals

◆ *Research*—to develop, evaluate, and monitor innovative strategies for community collaboration

◆ *Board communication*—to keep the board informed on the implemented strategies, results of community involvement efforts, and any potential policies needed

Committee Structure

The chair of the committee shall be a member of the board of directors and shall select, or cause to be selected, a vice chair. The chair and vice chair shall also serve as members of the executive committee, and shall keep the board informed on the committee's oversight of board-approved, committee goals. A majority of the committee shall be board members. Subcommittees or short-term task force groups may be formed to complete the committee's objectives.

Time Commitment

The time commitment is at least one meeting per month or as needed to fulfill the committee's goals.

(Note: In smaller communities, consolidation of Program and Community Involvement Committees is feasible.)

Committee Chair

Reports to, Selected, and Evaluated by

Board of Directors

Term

The term is one year, from election at the annual meeting until the next annual meeting.

Attendance Requirements

As a member of the board of directors, the committee chair adheres to the same attendance requirements as a board member, with additional attendance at the executive committee meetings.

Responsibilities

◆ *Meeting facilitation*—serves as the facilitator of the committee meetings; may be asked to facilitate the executive committee or board meetings in the absence of the chair

◆ *Staff advisor*—acts as advisor to the designated staff between board meetings on relevant matters

◆ *Bylaws responsibilities*—from the bylaws, Article V, Sec. 6: "In the absence of the chair of the board or in the event of the chair's inability or refusal to act, a vice chair shall be appointed to perform the duties of chair of the board and, when so acting, shall have all the powers of and be subject to all the restrictions upon the chair of the board. Committee chairs of the board shall serve as vice chairs of the board. The committee chairs of the board shall perform such other duties as from time to time may be assigned to them by the chair of the board or by the board of directors."

Commitment

◆ To facilitate all meetings in a neutral manner, encouraging input and participation by everyone in attendance

◆ To provide leadership to the committee and assure adherence to the policies, ethics, values, vision, and mission of the organization when developing recommendations for the board or staff

◆ To provide appropriate evaluation and recognition of staff and volunteer efforts within the committee

Time Commitment

In addition to the board member time commitment, approximately four hours per quarter is required for advisory duties to staff, facilitation of committee meeting, attendance at executive committee meetings, and monitoring of volunteer efforts related to the designated committee.

Vice Chair of Committee

Reports to, Selected, and Evaluated by

Board of Directors

Term

The term is one year, from election at the annual meeting until the next annual meeting.

Attendance Requirements

As a member of the board of directors, the committee vice chair adheres to the same attendance requirements as a board member, with additional attendance at the executive committee meetings.

Responsibilities

◆ *Meeting facilitation*—serves as the facilitator of the committee meetings in the absence of the committee chair and may be asked to facilitate the executive committee or board meetings in the absence of the board chair or committee chair

◆ *Leadership development*—to assimilate historical, policy, and procedural information with a goal toward potential additional leadership within the organization

◆ *Bylaws responsibilities*—from the bylaws, Article V, Sec. 1: "The officers of the corporation shall be a chair of the board, committee chairs, committee vice chairs. . ."; Article V, Sec. 6: "In the absence of the chair of the board or in the event of his/her inability or refusal to act, a vice chair shall be appointed to perform the duties of chair of the board, and when so acting, shall have all the powers of and be subject to all the restrictions upon the chair of the board. committee vice chairs of the board shall serve as vice chairs of the committees of the corporation. the committee vice chairs of the board shall perform such other duties as from time to time may be assigned to them by the chair of the board, the committee chair, or by the board of directors."

Commitment

◆ To facilitate, when asked, all meetings in a neutral manner, encouraging input and participation by everyone in attendance

◆ To observe the leadership to the committee and assure adherence to the policies, ethics, values, vision, and mission of the organization when developing recommendations for the board or staff

◆ To support the committee chair as needed

Time Commitment

In addition to the board member time commitment, approximately three hours per quarter is required as needed for attendance at executive committee meeting and interaction with the committee chair and designated staff.

Appendix D—Core Elements Assessment

Board and staff members should place a check mark beside each standard they know the nonprofit meets or exceeds. Return only the last page to _____ by the deadline indicated in the cover letter. Be sure your name is on the last page before sending to the consultant or ED, so your copy can be returned to you after tallying.

Standards/Benchmarks

✓	I. Basic Infrastructure
	A. Vision/Mission/Values
	1. The organization has a board-approved vision statement.
	2. The vision statement is no more than twenty-five words, contains no action words but states the ideal, ultimate goal of the organization. It answers the question, "Why does the organization exist?"
	3. The vision statement is reviewed by the board and staff at least every other year.
	4. The organization has a board-approved mission statement.
	5. The mission statement is short (twenty-five words or fewer), concise, and clearly understood.
	6. The mission statement includes action words that answer the question, "What will the nonprofit do to achieve the vision?"
	7. The current programs of the nonprofit accurately reflect the mission statement.
	8. The mission statement is reviewed by the board and staff at least every other year.
	9. The nonprofit has a board-approved values or ethics statement included in relevant marketing materials and is posted in the organization's facilities.

B. Organizational Structure

1. An organizational chart shows a workable relationship between staff, volunteers, the board of directors, and board committees.

2. The board committees include oversight of all of the core elements: administration, board/volunteer development, resource development, marketing, programs, community involvement.

3. The organization is, or is under the management of, an organization incorporated and exempt from federal income tax (under the provision of Section 501c of the Internal Revenue code) and has complied with all state and local codes.

C. Strategic Planning

1. The nonprofit annually examines internal trends, community trends, and national trends (social, philanthropic, political, and economic) to plan for the future.

2. The board annually develops realistic short- and long-range goals consistent with the organization's vision, mission, and values and which encompass all aspects of the organization.

3. There are written, measurable objectives and time frames for achieving them.

4. Implementation of the objectives is assigned to specific staff, volunteers, and/or committees.

5. The organization at least annually evaluates its programs, based on objectives, work plans, and outcome measures.

6. The board periodically plans and conducts a management audit of all internal and external operations, including the operations of the board and incorporates the audit into the planning process.

7. A variety of evaluation and assessment strategies are included in the organization's planning process and include identification of deficiencies and recommendations for correcting them.

8. Board members, staff, volunteers, and community stakeholders participate in the annual review and evaluation of the organization.

9. Total quality management is a board-approved operational procedure and philosophy, which is incorporated into the strategic plan.

10. The primary customer of the organization has been identified and ways to provide and measure top quality customer service have been implemented.

✓	II. Core Element—Administration
	A. Policies and procedures
	1. All legal documents are easily accessible when needed by staff or volunteers.
	2. A document checklist indicates the location of all legal documents.
	3. A policies and procedures manual is available for all staff and board members.
	4. The policies and procedures manual is updated at least annually.
	B. Financial
	1. The board has assigned financial oversight to a board standing committee, which presents easily understandable, written financial reports to the board at least quarterly.
	2. At least two signatures are required on all checks over a designated amount.
	3. Consecutive, numbered receipts are given out with all cash contributions.
	4. The annual budget is developed by staff, presented to the Finance Committee, approved by the board.
	5. Treasurer's reports include balance sheets.
	6. Treasurer's reports include amounts budgeted, amounts received and expended, and the variances, both monthly (or quarterly) and year-to-date.
	7. The board regularly evaluates its investment and banking policies to ensure the best possible management of the organization's funds.
	8. A certified audit is performed annually by an independent auditor (If the annual budget is below $100,000, a financial review is acceptable).
	9. The annual audit is unqualified, or if qualified, a plan to resolve the problems is presented to the board by the ED.
	10. A management letter from the CPA is provided and includes suggestions for improvements in the internal management of the nonprofit.
	11. The auditor includes a review of the accounting system in the yearly audit.
	12. The accounting books or computerized system are easily accessible to the board and are located in the organization's office in a secure location.

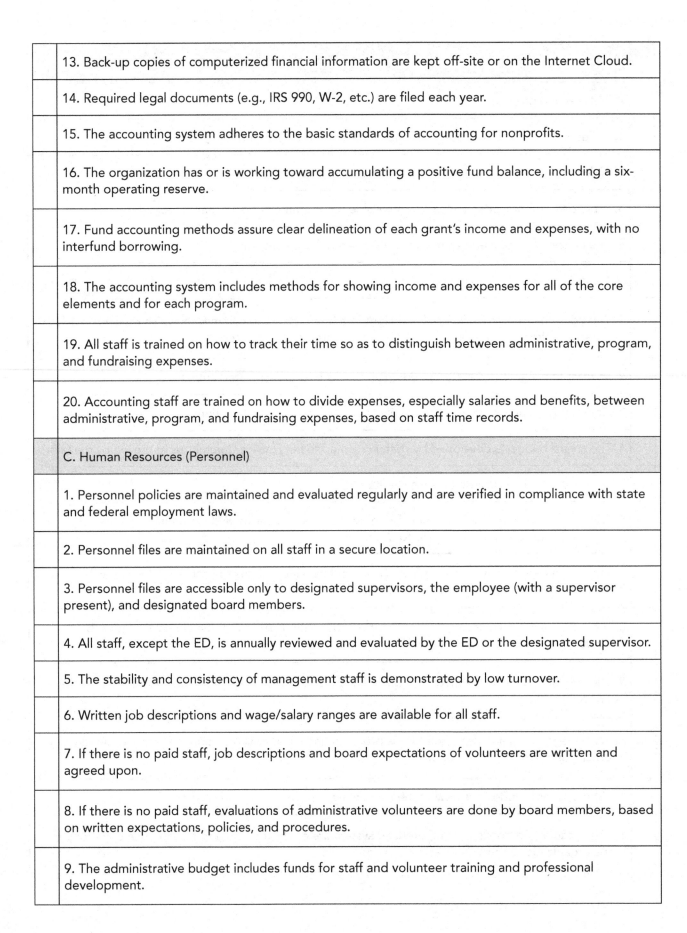

13. Back-up copies of computerized financial information are kept off-site or on the Internet Cloud.

14. Required legal documents (e.g., IRS 990, W-2, etc.) are filed each year.

15. The accounting system adheres to the basic standards of accounting for nonprofits.

16. The organization has or is working toward accumulating a positive fund balance, including a six-month operating reserve.

17. Fund accounting methods assure clear delineation of each grant's income and expenses, with no interfund borrowing.

18. The accounting system includes methods for showing income and expenses for all of the core elements and for each program.

19. All staff is trained on how to track their time so as to distinguish between administrative, program, and fundraising expenses.

20. Accounting staff are trained on how to divide expenses, especially salaries and benefits, between administrative, program, and fundraising expenses, based on staff time records.

C. Human Resources (Personnel)

1. Personnel policies are maintained and evaluated regularly and are verified in compliance with state and federal employment laws.

2. Personnel files are maintained on all staff in a secure location.

3. Personnel files are accessible only to designated supervisors, the employee (with a supervisor present), and designated board members.

4. All staff, except the ED, is annually reviewed and evaluated by the ED or the designated supervisor.

5. The stability and consistency of management staff is demonstrated by low turnover.

6. Written job descriptions and wage/salary ranges are available for all staff.

7. If there is no paid staff, job descriptions and board expectations of volunteers are written and agreed upon.

8. If there is no paid staff, evaluations of administrative volunteers are done by board members, based on written expectations, policies, and procedures.

9. The administrative budget includes funds for staff and volunteer training and professional development.

	10. The organization has a written affirmative action policy that clearly states it will operate without discrimination in the selection of board members, volunteers, and committee members and in the employment of staff in all protected classes, such as age, sex, ethnicity, religion, and sexual orientation.
	11. A formal process is established and followed for the annual review or evaluation of the ED by the board.
D. Facilities & Equipment	
	1. Facilities and equipment are maintained in a neat and orderly manner.
	2. Facilities and equipment are appropriate to the mission.
	3. Facilities, equipment, and overall atmosphere contribute to staff and volunteer safety, enthusiasm, and production and are ergonomically correct and handicapped accessible when required by law.
	4. The board has a policy for procurement, maintenance, and replacement of equipment.
E. Risk Management	
	1. Employee benefits include unlimited major medical, disability, and life insurance.
	2. An employee or volunteer committee annually evaluates health and safety issues related to the facility, the grounds, and equipment that can negatively impact employees, staff, volunteers, clients, etc.
	3. The nonprofit has internal and external disaster plans; volunteers and staff are trained how to respond.
	4. Directors and officers liability insurance is included in the budget.
	5. General liability insurance for staff and volunteers is adequate to meet the risks of the programs.
	6. The state's Good Samaritan laws are annually reviewed to verify compliance by the nonprofit.
	7. Policies and procedures clearly outline prevention and response strategies for all risky behavior by staff, volunteers, clients, or the public, such as sexual harassment, domestic violence, substance abuse, client abuse, etc.
	8. Property insurance is included in the budget.
	9. The board at least annually evaluates whether time, crime, automobile, or other insurance is needed.
	10. Workers compensation insurance is included in the budget.
	11. Crisis communication policies state who speaks for the organization, when they speak, and the process for developing statements to the press.

III. Core Element—Board and Volunteer Development
A. Board of Directors
1. The board of directors has a minimum of ten active members.
2. When multiple geographical areas are served by the nonprofit, volunteer advisory boards are established with clear lines of communication to the board of directors.
3. The board of directors meets at least quarterly.
4. At least 50 percent of the board members regularly attend all board meetings.
5. Terms of office for the board of directors are clearly stated in the bylaws with no board member allowed to serve more than two consecutive terms.
6. No more than one staff person (the ED) serves as an ex-officio, nonvoting board member, and the ED does not serve as chair of the board.
7. Agendas are prepared and mailed ahead of time for board and committee meetings, with input from the committee chair and the designated staff person.
8. Standing committees meet regularly and report to the full board at each meeting.
9. Minutes of all board and executive committee meetings are kept in an easily accessible location, with the minutes of the previous meeting available at each meeting.
10. Board members are trained in their roles, responsibilities, lines of authority (in relationship to staff), and on how to conduct effective meetings.
11. At the beginning of each term, board members sign commitment to serve, confidentiality, and conflict of interest statements.
12. Succession plans are in place for all officers of the board.
B. Volunteer Development
1. The nonprofit has written, board-approved policies for the recruitment, training, recognition, and dismissal of all volunteers: board, committee, and program.
2. All volunteers and staff understand their roles and responsibilities, including legal and personal liabilities, and lines of authority.
3. The demographics of all volunteers reflect the communities served.
4. Job descriptions are available for all volunteer positions.

	5. A board-level committee is responsible for oversight of the volunteer development policies and procedures for all volunteers, including nominations of board members and officers.
✓	**IV. Core Element—Programs**
	1. The services/programs of the nonprofit adhere to the mission statement.
	2. All services/programs are provided without bias and in a nonpartisan manner.
	3. Political and religious activities are avoided, except to the extent allowed by law.
	4. Cooperative efforts with other nonprofits are evident.
	5. The organization has an ongoing process for examining and adapting programs to changing customer/client and community needs.
	6. No program is started until a plan has been presented to the board that includes why the program is needed, how it will be implemented, the resources needed, the expected length of the program, and evaluation and outcomes measurements methods for program effectiveness.
	7. Distribution of funds to programs and strategies are periodically examined for possible updating or improvement.
	8. Resource and needs assessments are used in the development of program priorities.
	9. All programs are evaluated at least annually, using pre-determined indicators and outcomes measurements, with the results of the evaluations presented first to the board-level program committee and then to the board.
	V. Core Element—Community Involvement
	1. Staff is encouraged to be involved in community organizations to increase awareness of the nonprofit and its programs and to better understand other programs and services available to their customers/clients.
	2. The nonprofit plays a significant role in the community as the expert in a specific program area.
	3. The nonprofit can demonstrate cooperative efforts with business, government, education, health agencies, other nonprofits, faith-based organizations, and unions.
✓	**VI. Core Element—Resource Development**
	1. The board has approved an anti-coercion policy for fundraising.
	2. Fund raising strategies and results are examined after each fundraising project, with recommendations incorporated into the next effort.
	3. Fund raising strategies are used that will generate an 80 percent income and no more than 20 percent in expenses (including staff costs).

	4. No more than 20 percent of the budget comes from any single source or fundraising strategy.
	5. Board members are involved in fundraising.
	6. Board members are required to make a financial contribution to the nonprofit commiserate with their personal income level.
	7. Staff involved in fundraising regularly attends fundraising workshops to gather new ideas and expertise.
	8. Fundraising strategies are based on research that indicates the pros and cons of each strategy.
	9. A long-term, planned giving program is in effect.
	10. A variety of fundraising strategies are used.
	11. To avoid burnout of volunteers and staff, no more than three fundraising events are conducted within one year.
✓	**VII. Core Element—Marketing**
	1. An annual, year-round marketing plan is being implemented.
	2. Marketing plans are based on a specific brand image the nonprofit wants conveyed.
	3. All publications and marketing materials consistently convey a message that enhances the mission.
	4. Marketing strategies are based on research.
	5. Marketing and publicity strategies use proven outcomes measurements of the programs to tell the "story" of the mission of the nonprofit.

Summary of Assessment

Enter the number of check marks you made for each category.

Number of Checks	Maximum Number	Category
		I. Basic Infrastructure
	9	Vision/mission/values
	3	Organizational structure
	10	Strategic planning
		II. Core Element—Administration
	4	Policies and procedures

Number of Checks	Maximum Number	Category
	20	Financial
	11	Human resources (personnel)
	4	Facilities and equipment
	11	Risk management
		III. Core Element—Board/Volunteer Development
	12	Board of directors
	5	Volunteer development
	9	IV. Core Element—Programs
	3	V. Core Element—Community Involvement
	11	VI. Core Element—Resource Development
	5	VII. Core Element—Marketing

Return this completed page to _____ **by the deadline in the cover letter or e-mail.**

Name_____ **Board Member** ☐ **Staff** ☐

Appendix E—Strategic Planning Forms

Goal Setting Form

Complete one form for each goal.

20___ to 20___

Nonprofit: _____

Date: _____

Committee (check which committee is completing this form):

☐ Marketing ☐ Resource Development ☐ Program ☐ Community Involvement

☐ Administration ☐ Volunteer and Board Development

List Committee Members:

_____

_____

_____

_____

Priority Issues:

List in priority order, based on the results of the number of dots each received.

1. _____

2. _____

3. _____

4. _____

5. _____

6. _____

7. _____

8. _____

For each priority issue, complete the following information:

Goal (include an expected outcome and completion date in the goal statement like the sample one-page strategic plan): _____

_____

_____

Environmental/contextual issues that impact the goal: _____

_____

_____

Barriers that may hinder goal completion and possible solutions: _____

_____

_____

List at least three strategies that could be used to complete the goal (*Think outside the norm.*): _____

_____

_____

Identify the most workable strategy, given the organization's resources: _____

_____

_____

Who will be responsible for implementing the strategy?

Board Member:_____

Program Volunteer:_____

Staff: _____

What is the most realistic date for completion of the goal?_____

How will the outcomes of the goal be evaluated or measured? _____

_____

_____

List the specific action steps, timelines, and responsible individual for each step necessary to complete the goal:

Action Steps	Due Date	Who is Responsible?
_____	_____	_____
_____	_____	_____
_____	_____	_____
_____	_____	_____

Strategic Planning Impact Forms

I. Program Plan

To be completed annually by the program staff. . . one form for each program. The same format can be used for evaluation of proposed programs.

Person Submitting the Plan: _____

Date: _____

Program Name: _____

Rationale for the Program (Vision or "why" the program exists): _____

_____

_____

Mission (or "what" the program will do): _____

_____

_____

Goal or Outcomes Measurement (How will you know the program is successful?): _____

_____

_____

Start Date: _____

Age Group: _____

Number of Clients: _____

Transportation Needs: _____

Lead Staff: _____

Number of Volunteers: _____

Hours of Operation: _____

Location: _____

Annual Budget (per month): _____

Expenses: _____

Income: _____

Marketing Strategies: _____

_____

_____

Legal or Insurance issues: _____

_____

_____

List any challenges or threats to the program: _____

_____

_____

Why should this program be started/continued or eliminated? ____

_____

_____

II. Strategic Analysis

Use this form anytime there is an unexpected challenge or an issue that arises or there are proposed changes or additions of programs that will impact the nonprofit.

Answer all relevant questions and present a written report to the designated board-level committee for consideration. Include a program plan if the analysis is about a proposed addition or elimination of a program.

Person submitting the report:_____

Date:_____

How does the proposal or challenge support our vision and mission or impact them?_____

What are the leadership, volunteer, staffing, or other personnel challenges?_____

What are the operational implications?_____

What are the expenses? (Include all staffing, implementation, and facility costs, etc.)_____

Where will the income come from to cover costs? (Include potential sources such as client fees, grants, etc.)_____

_____

What are the legal and insurance implications?_____

_____

What are the demographic rationales?_____

_____

What are the statistical reasons for the challenge or issue to be evaluated?_____

_____

How will this issue impact our marketing and resource development strategies?_____

_____

What are the competitive issues? _____

_____

Are there are other nonprofits addressing the issue or challenge and how will our approach differ or enhance their efforts?_____

_____

How will this issue impact our unique role in the community?_____

_____

How will this issue or challenge impact our future growth?_____

_____

How does this fit with our strategic plan and how will it change the strategic plan?_____

_____

What are the positive and negative impacts of the issue?_____

_____

What is your recommendation? (State in one sentence and include an outcomes measurement: How will we know we have addressed the issue?)_____

_____

_____

Strategic Planning Workshop Evaluation Form

To improve our strategic planning process, complete this form and submit it to the facilitator or the ED before you leave today. At the end of each statement, indicated your rating of the agenda item or process. Add any suggestions you might have for improvement. All ratings are based on a 1–5 scale, 5 = excellent and 1 = poor.

1. Core elements as a tool for organizational structure and evaluation of the nonprofit:_____

2. Vision and mission statement development process:_____

3. ED's environmental assessment:_____

4. Standards of excellence assessment: _____

5. SWOT (strengths, weaknesses, opportunities, and threats) analysis: _____

6. Prioritizing of the issues (colored dots): _____

7. Committee development of goals/objectives and outcomes measurements: _____

8. Program planning form: _____

9. Strategic analysis questions and form: _____

10. Location, facility, breaks, meal: _____

11. Facilitator: _____

12. Overall ranking for the entire six-hour session: _____

Thank you for your participation today!

Appendix F—Meeting Checklist for Facilitators or Committee Chairpersons

Set-up

- ❑ Have I clearly defined the purpose of the meeting?

- ❑ Are there alternative issues that need to be researched prior to the meeting?

- ❑ What objectives need to be accomplished?

- ❑ Who needs to attend the meeting and have they been notified?

- ❑ When and where is the meeting scheduled? Are the facilities reserved and prepared?

- ❑ Have materials been prepared for the meeting? Were agendas and minutes mailed out (or e-mailed)?

- ❑ Are all needed items for discussion/action listed on the agenda?

Conducting the Meeting

- ❑ Did the meeting start on time?

- ❑ Did we stick to the agenda?

- ❑ Were the issues to be considered stated clearly?

- ❑ Did we follow orderly process (motions, discussions, and voting)?

- ❑ Did I invite discussion but not encourage debate?

- ❑ Did I keep attention focused on the problem at hand?

- ❑ Did I secure participation from each member?

- ❑ Did we all retain a sense of humor?

- ❑ Did I show appreciation for volunteer input and effort?

❑ Did I preserve an informal atmosphere?

❑ Did I avoid playing the school teacher?

❑ Did I keep discussion alive until all points were covered?

❑ Did I direct group thinking but provide an atmosphere for open discussion?

❑ Did I summarize from time to time?

❑ Did someone record all ideas and conclusions in minutes form?

❑ Did we stop on time?

❑ Did we handle conflict in an accepting and rational way?

❑ Was the next meeting and agenda discussed?

❑ Were responsibilities assigned for specific tasks?

Follow-up

❑ How should we evaluate the results of meeting?

❑ When is the next meeting?

❑ Are there unfinished matters?

❑ Have the minutes been typed and the date set for mailing to members?

Action Items

◆ What tasks are assigned to the chairperson/facilitator?

◆ Does chairperson need to follow up with members on assigned tasks?

◆ Do any policies need to be written and taken to the board for approval?

◆ Do any changes need to be made in the way the next meeting is conducted?

◆ Do any participants need special thank you as a result of their involvement in the meeting?

Appendix G—Sample Board Meeting Minutes

The sample minutes are based on the sample agenda. The numbers in parenthesis indicate the page number of attachments.

*M/S/P (motion made, seconded, passed)

Date:

Present:

Board Members: Joe Jones, Susie Brown, Ed Smith, etc.
Staff: Julie Joy, etc.
Guests: Jim Jordan

Absent:

Board Members: Jim Douglas, etc.

Consent Agenda:

The following consent agenda items were approved (*M/S/P):

(Copies of these items will be included with the final, approved copy of these minutes.)

- ◆ Minutes of the last meeting (#2)

- ◆ ED report (#3–4)

- ◆ Executive committee minutes (#5)

- ◆ Signatory changes on bank account (#6)

- ◆ Committee reports (#7–12)

October Financial Report (M/S/P):

Questions were raised about the reason why line item six was over budget. The finance committee chair, Joe Jones, stated this was a one-time expense and will be covered by the grant approved last month.

Old Business:

The October fundraiser showed a 15 percent increase over last year (#17). The resource development committee will appoint the planning committee for the next fundraiser at their next meeting.

The revised marketing plan for 2012 (#18–19) was approved (M/S/P) and will be implemented by staff.

The revised policy related to D&O insurance (#20) was approved (M/S/P, Joe Jones voting nay). The ED will contact the insurance company about the changes.

New Business:

The ED presented a new chart that will show quarterly the progress toward achievement of strategic goals approved at the last meeting (#21).

The audit for the 2011 finances will be conducted by the Carson & Castle accounting firm. A three-year audit contract (#22–25) was approved (M/S/P). Susie Jones was not in the room during the discussion and did not vote because of a declared conflict of interest as a member of the accounting firm.

Because of the Christmas holiday, there will be no meeting in December. The next meeting will be on 1/27/12.

Meeting adjourned (M/S/P) at 1:15 pm.

Appendix H—Sample Executive Director Core Competencies

A Self-awareness Assessment

Score yourself in each area with 1–10, 10 being the best and 1 being no knowledge in this area. After completing the assessment, total your scores. This assessment is a guide to assist an ED in identifying areas needing improvement and is not a scientific or complete assessment tool. This can also be used as a tool for the ED performance review.

Provides Leadership

- ❑ fosters the development of a common vision for the nonprofit among volunteers, board, staff, and the community
- ❑ provides clear direction and sense of priorities
- ❑ makes tough, courageous decisions
- ❑ creates energy and enthusiasm.
- ❑ guides the board and key committees in policy formulation and interpretation
- ❑ understands the legal requirements for nonprofit management
- ❑ is able to adapt management style to fit the needs of the nonprofit
- ❑ mobilizes the staff and volunteers for action

Score:_____

Catalyst for Strategic Planning

- ❑ understands changing social, economic, religious, and political climates
- ❑ develops innovative program approaches to meet trends; acts as catalyst for needed change and strategic planning among board, staff, and the community

❏ is able to make changes in management approach to fit changes in demographics and nonprofit needs

Score: _____

Skilled at Resource Development

❏ is able to develop and lead effective resource development strategies

❏ has personal ability to make fundraising appeals

❏ is adept at in-kind and planned giving resource development strategies

Score: _____

Relationship Builder

❏ establishes open, trusting, and candid working relationships with all stakeholders

❏ treats everyone fairly and with respect

❏ demonstrates commitment to diversity objectives

❏ deals constructively with conflicts and difficult people

❏ is able to effectively deal with the volunteers, staff, and clients

❏ builds consensus and a credible image to the community

Score: _____

Encourages Volunteer Involvement

❏ understands and puts into action volunteer recruitment, training, recognition, and dismissal strategies for board members, program volunteers, and committee volunteers

❏ skilled at bringing diverse people together and mobilizing them for mission fulfillment

❏ handles well the paradox of leading and being led by volunteers

Score: _____

Effective Communicator

❏ articulates well both verbally and in writing

❏ listens well

❏ encourages differing ideas and opinions

❏ presentations are well organized and understandable

❏ promotes communication throughout the nonprofit

❏ understands importance of effective marketing of all aspects of the program to both volunteers and the community

❑ adjusts communication techniques to the various stakeholders

Score: _____

Mature Self-confidence

❑ has a positive outlook

❑ is able to handle stress constructively

❑ knows own strengths and weaknesses

❑ has clear sense of personal passion and direction

❑ is a constant learner

❑ seeks feedback

❑ has high standards of personal integrity

❑ is able to juggle demands of nonprofit and personal life

Score: _____

Provides Effective Staff Leadership

❑ attracts high-caliber employees

❑ creates effective organizational structure

❑ makes tough staffing decisions

❑ supports and encourages staff

❑ understands and implements good, legal personnel strategies and policies that meet state and federal labor laws

❑ focuses on results and measures staff on outcomes

❑ strives to achieve staff diversity

❑ coaches staff

❑ provides a learning and personal growth environment

❑ creates passion in staff for mission achievement

Score: _____

Financial and Resource Management Skills

❑ understands budget development and implementation

❑ manages resources wisely

❑ develops and maintains strong financial controls based on basic standards of accounting for nonprofits

❑ is able to convey financial information in an easily-understood format to the volunteers, staff, and community

❑ understands facilities, equipment, and risk management issues, such as insurance needs, disaster preparedness, and safety

Score: _____

Demonstrates Commitment to Ethics and Values

❑ possesses a passion for serving people

❑ is committed to the vision, mission, values, and goals of the nonprofit

❑ understands and implements strategies to fulfill the vision, mission, and goals

❑ works well with colleagues

❑ is able to deal with conflict within the nonprofit

Score: _____

Skilled at Community Building and Collaboration

❑ understands and reacts to the wider community issues

❑ is a collaborator rather than believing the nonprofit is the only way to address community resources and needs

❑ works to promote nonprofit and community involvement rather than focusing only internally

Score: _____

Understands Legal Issues

❑ is able to assure the nonprofit meets all legal requirements, including any federal, state, or local tax and/or document filing issues

❑ understands the legal responsibilities of the board

❑ has knowledge of Americans with Disabilities Act requirements

Score: _____

Able to Measure Effectiveness of each Program

❑ understands outcomes measurements and able to track effectiveness of programs and to make recommendations for changes where needed

❑ has the ability to juggle differences in stakeholder desires and the needs of clients and the community

❑ understands and incorporates ethnic and demographic differences into programs.

Score: _____

Total Score _____

97–130 = Well-equipped for the ED position

65–96 = Satisfactory but needs improvement in some areas

43–64 = Needs improvement in a significant number of areas

1–42 = Prompt training and/or assistance needed

Appendix I—Sample Executive Director Job Description

Executive Director

Responsible to

The direct supervisor of the ED shall be the chair of the board, but the ED is responsible to the board for fulfillment of board-approved job objectives.

Key responsibilities

The ED shall be responsible for, or cause to be implemented, all internal and external operations of the nonprofit and the fulfillment of all board-approved policies, including:

- *Management and general*—oversight of the staff or volunteers in charge of all Internal Management of the nonprofit, such as financial controls, accounting, adherence to legal requirements and reports, payroll, staff supervision, strategic planning, technology development, risk management, etc.

- *Volunteer/board management*—oversight of the staff or volunteers responsible for the implementation of all volunteer recruitment, recognition, training, and dismissal procedures, which will utilize the skills and expertise of the volunteers in the most effective manner possible for all aspects of the nonprofit; understands the roles, responsibilities, and lines of authority for all types of volunteers (board, committee, and program)

- *Program management*—oversight of the staff or volunteers responsible for the development and implementation of all programs approved by the board

- *Community involvement*—oversight of the volunteers or staff responsible for all aspects of community involvement and community collaboration

- *Marketing*—oversight of staff or volunteers responsible for the development and implementation of a year-round marketing plan, publicity campaigns, and all aspects of building brand identity and positive public relations

- *Resource development*—oversight of the volunteers or staff involved in all aspects of resource development, fundraising, and planned giving for the nonprofit

Skills Required

The ED should score high in all of the core competencies, have the ability to work effectively with the board and volunteers, be an excellent communicator (both verbal and written), and possess a working knowledge of resource development, financial management, and program development.

Education Required

The ED should have a bachelor's degree or master's degree equivalent with emphasis on nonprofit management; minimum of three to five years of experience as ED.

Salary Range

$60,000 to $100,000, depending on experience

Appendix J—Sample Executive Director Performance Review

Executive Director:_____

Date of Review:_____ **Hire Date:** _____

Review done by: ☐ Board Member ☐ ED ☐ Other ☐ Staff

Scoring: 1 = performance does not meet job requirements, 5 = performance exceeds job requirements

Achievement of Nonprofit Objectives

Based on a review of the nonprofit's objectives for the year (copy attached), indicate your analysis of the ED's achievement areas:

High-Achievement Areas: _____

_____

Areas Needing Improvement: _____

_____

Total Performance Score on Achievement of Nonprofit Objectives:_____

Managerial Effectiveness

Based on your knowledge and actual experience, indicate your analysis of the ED's managerial effectiveness. If you do not have first-hand knowledge of a specific area, leave it blank. A copy of the ED's job description is attached for you to use for comparison.

A. Management and general: Overall management of internal management _____

B. Volunteer management: Implementation of volunteer recruitment, training, dismissal, and recognition strategies (including governing board) _____

C. Program management: Oversight of all programs _____

D. Community involvement: Representation of the nonprofit to the community in a community-building methodology _____

E. Marketing: Leadership in development and implementation of all marketing strategies _____

F. Resource development: Management of all fundraising, gifts-in-kind, and planned giving strategies _____

Total Management Effectiveness Score: _____

Use of Core Competencies' Skills

In what ways did the ED demonstrate skilled use of the Core Competencies (copy attached)? List specific examples:

A. Provides leadership_____

_____

_____

B. Catalyst for strategic planning_____

_____

_____

C. Skilled at resource development _____

_____

_____

D. Relationship builder_____

_____

_____

E. Encourages volunteer involvement_____

_____

_____

F. Effective communicator_____

_____

_____

G. Mature self-confidence_____

_____

_____

H. Provides effective staff leadership_____

_____

_____

I. Financial and resource management skills_____

_____

_____

J. Demonstrates commitment to nonprofit values and doctrines_____

_____

_____

K. Skilled at community building and collaboration_____

_____

_____

Total Core Competencies Score: _____

Performance Summary

1. Total score on achievement of nonprofit objectives _____

2. Total score on management effectiveness _____

3. Total score on core competencies _____

Overall Score: _____

("90" is the highest possible score)

Index

CPSIA information can be obtained
at www.ICGtesting.com
Printed in the USA
FSOW03n1326120117
29513FS

9 781938 077784